A VELVET REVOLUTION

VÁCLAV HAVEL

AND THE FALL OF COMMUNISM

A VELVET REVOLUTION

VÁCLAV HAVEL

AND THE FALL OF COMMUNISM

John Duberstein

**MORGAN
REYNOLDS**

PUBLISHING

Greensboro, North Carolina

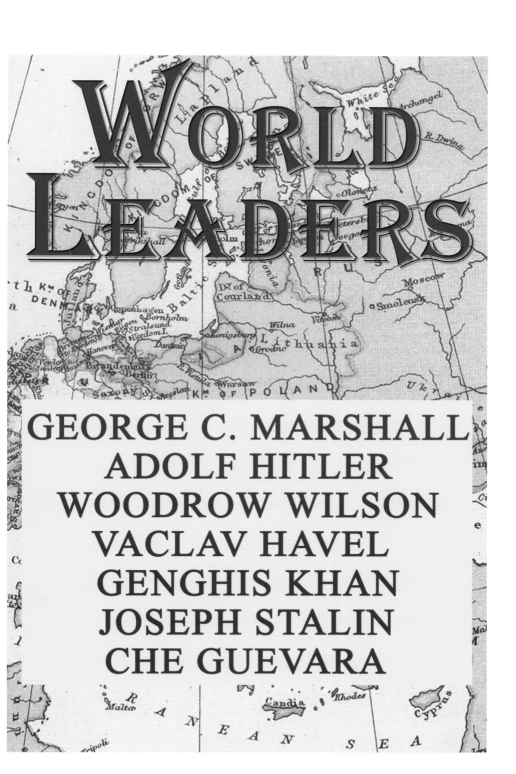

WORLD LEADERS

GEORGE C. MARSHALL
ADOLF HITLER
WOODROW WILSON
VACLAV HAVEL
GENGHIS KHAN
JOSEPH STALIN
CHE GUEVARA

A VELVET REVOLUTION: VACLAV HAVEL
AND THE FALL OF COMMUNISM

Copyright © 2006 by John Duberstein

Library of Congress Cataloging-in-Publication Data

Duberstein, John, 1976-
   A velvet revolution : Václav Havel and the fall of communism /
John Duberstein.— 1st ed. p. cm.
   Includes bibliographical references and index.
   ISBN-13: 978-1-931798-85-3 (library binding)
   ISBN-10: 1-931798-85-0 (library binding)
   1. Havel, Václav. 2. Presidents—Czechoslovakia—Biography. 3.
Dissenters—Czechoslovakia—Biography. 4. Dramatists, Czech—
20th century—Biography. 5. Czechoslovakia—Politics and govern-
ment—1968-1989. 6. Czech Republic—Politics and government—
1993- I. Title.
   DB2241.H38D83 2006
   943.704'3092—dc22

                              2006000008

Printed in the United States of America
First Edition

To my father
Allen Duberstein
1942-2005

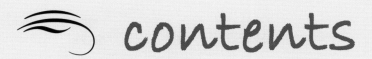 contents

Václav Havel. (Courtesy of Getty Images.)

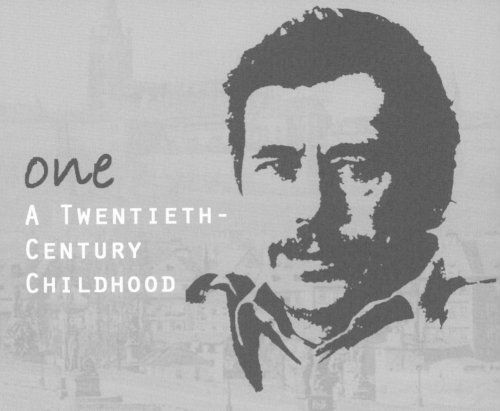

one
A Twentieth-Century Childhood

From the beginning, Václav Havel's life was filled with dramatic changes. He was born on Monday, October 5, 1936, in a private hospital to a prosperous middle-class family. He was the first born child of Václav M. Havel and Bozena Havlová.

Havel was born in the bustling city of Prague, the capital of what is now the Czech Republic. Prague had also been the home of Franz Kafka, the writer whose unsettling works strangely prophesied the often absurd and treacherous world that Havel would be forced to live in most of his life. But unlike in a Kafka tale, in which the hero is usually victimized by an absurd society, Havel would eventually emerge intact from both Nazi and Communist totalitarianism.

Built along the Vltava River, below a majestic castle

Prague's National Theater, opened in 1881, is one of the great symbols of the rich artistic tradition that defines Czech culture. (Library of Congress)

where Czech rulers had lived for over 1000 years, the Prague of Havel's youth was a city of legendary beauty. It had been dubbed the "Paris of Central Europe," because of its varied and beautiful architecture, vibrant cafés, many restaurants, and rich cultural life. Prague was filled with theaters, lush green spaces, modern roadways, and luxury shopping.

Vanousek, as the infant Václav was nicknamed to distinguish him from his father, was born into a family of builders. His grandfather had built the famous Lucerna entertainment complex, the first concrete and steel structure in Prague. His father was a civil engineer who built Barrandov, a ritzy suburban development just outside the capital city. The Havels were friends with many influential people. They supported the Czechoslovak Republic formed after World War I and the democratic, humanist principles it represented. Friends of the family included prominent politicians, writers, and philosophers. Tomás Masaryk, the first president of the Czechoslovak Republic, was a friend of Havel's grandfather.

At Václav's birth, servants on the family estate sent their best wishes and asked that the infant bestow his favor upon them in the future. Early photos of Havel show a sandy-haired boy surrounded by toys, family friends, and his aristocratic-looking mother. Bozena, a beautiful woman from a respected Czech family, was educated, graceful, and very involved with the education and development of her sons.

Vanousek was born at a difficult juncture in European and Czech history. The two main ethnic groups in Czechoslovakia, the Czechs and Slovaks, had always been neighbors, but had distinct histories, cultures, and languages. They were both Slavic peoples, their language was part of the same family that includes Russian, Ukrainian, and Serbo-Croatian, among others, and both had been subjects of the Austro-Hungarian Empire, which ruled over Eastern Europe for centuries until World War I.

The Czechs and Slovaks had formed a political union after World War I. Czechoslovakia joined the Czech lands with the more rural and mountainous Slovak region, which had only one city of any size, Bratislava, a provincial town even by regional standards. It was an

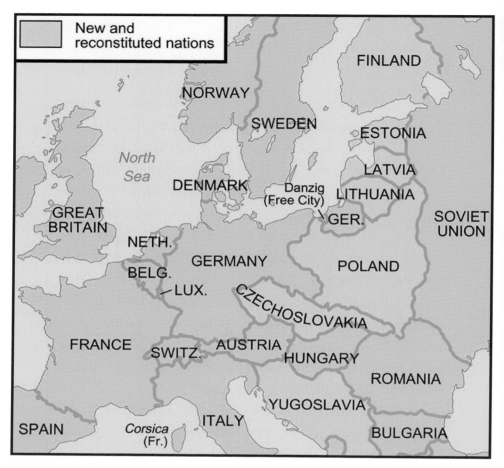

Europe as it looked in 1919, after the signing of the Versailles Treaty at the end of World War I.

uneasy marriage in some regards. The Slovaks felt looked down upon by the more cosmopolitan Czechs, who in turn resented their less prosperous and more countrified neighbors. The location of the capital in the Czech city of Prague did not help the Slovak inferiority complex. The two groups managed to agree on a union, in spite of their differences, partly because the international community at the time encouraged unification in an attempt to rebuild Europe after the war. Unfortunately, Europe had several more years of self-destruction in its future.

In September 1938 British prime minister Neville Chamberlain agreed to allow German Nazi leader Adolf Hitler to seize the Sudetenland, a part of the Czechoslovak Republic where many ethnic Germans lived. Hitler insisted it was his duty to annex this territory to protect the German minority. Czechoslovakia, which had been created by European leaders, was now being parceled out in a vain attempt to avert war.

After meeting with Hitler, in March of 1939, the third president of Czechoslovakia, Emil Hácha, called on the Czechoslovak people to embrace Czech-German "cooperation" and abandon all resistance to the German troops. German forces marched into Prague only hours after the meeting.

England and France had given the Nazis permission to turn the Czechoslovak Republic into a *Reichsprotektorat*, or dependency of the German Nazi Third Reich. Not only the Sudetenland, but also Bohemia and Moravia, the heart of the Czech lands, were seized. The Czech army and parliament were dissolved. All political parties other than the Nazi Party were banned. German citizens were given special privileges, including immunity from Czech courts.

Czechoslovakia now belonged to Hitler. The province of Ruthenia, meanwhile, was absorbed by Hungary— then a Nazi ally keen on recovering territory lost in World War I. Slovakia was separated as a semi-autonomous state under Nazi protection. Czechoslovakia was dismantled—almost literally—overnight.

A few months later, in September, the Nazis invaded Poland and World War II began. Europe, Asia, and eventually America were plunged into a global conflict that would pit the Axis powers (Germany, Italy, and Japan) against the Allies (primarily Britain, France, and eventually Russia and the United States). It would become the most destructive war of the twentieth century.

The Havels, prominent Czechs associated closely with the Republic, feared liquidation by the Nazis. They fled Prague for Havlov, the country estate the family owned in the eastern province of Moravia. Havlov was a half-wood, half-plaster villa with green window frames and a swimming pool, hidden in a small forest near a stream, and was an easy hike from a famous Czech castle. Here in the rural haven of Havlov, Bozena tried to raise Václav and his younger brother Ivan, born on October 11, 1938, as though everything was normal.

Havlov was situated near a village called Zd'arec. Václav was enrolled in a private school nearby. In September 1944, Ivan joined his older brother at school. Each day the boys walked together down the dirt road wearing the school uniform—white jackets and short pants—and carrying leather book bags.

The Havels' attempt to try to live peacefully amidst the fury of the war was not unusual. For the most part, Czechs did not put up much resistance to the Nazification process. One notable exception, and an event that also forms one of Václav Havel's most indelible early memories, was the assassination of Reinhard Heydrich, the

Eight-year-old Václav (left) *and his younger brother Ivan on their way to school.*
(Havel Family Archives)

S.S. leader in Czechoslovakia and one of the organizers
of the Final Solution that sent over six million Jews to
the death camps.

Václav was only six years old when, on May 27, 1942,
paratroopers, sent on the assassination mission by the
Czech government in exile in London, bombed Heydrich's
car. The S.S. leader died from infected wounds nine days
later. After the attack, Heinrich Himmler—the head of
the Nazi S.S.—ordered a search for Heydrich's assassins. Suspected of harboring the commandos, the village
of Lidice was liquidated in a cruel display of Nazi terror
tactics. The adult men were shot and the women were sent
to concentration camps, as were all the children not
deemed to possess "Aryan" traits. The Aryan-looking
ones—those with light-colored hair and eyes—were
adopted into German households. Lidice was then literally removed from the map, although the link between
the village and the assassination was never firmly established. Eventually, the assassins were cornered, but
they took their own lives before being apprehended.

Though Václav did not witness the devastation at
Lidice, the events affected all Czechs because of the
stringent and cruel measures the Nazis enforced in their
wake. The repression brought problems closer to the
Havel home when the Nazis persecuted Václav's favorite
uncle. Milos Havel was a film producer, openly homo-
sexual, and unwilling to capitulate to demands to produce Nazi propaganda films. His studio was eventually
seized, but fortunately for Milos and the rest of the

Not long after the Nazis razed Lidice, several towns in countries around the world renamed themselves in honor of the massacred village so that the name would live on despite the Nazi's intention. Lidice was eventually rebuilt in 1949. (Library of Congress)

Czech people, just as the deportations and other repressive measures were intensifying, the Nazis had to retreat west in the face of advancing Russian troops. The end of the Nazi occupation did not mean an end to the terror, however. Eight-year-old Václav sat huddled around a radio with his parents at Havlov, listening to the news as the final convulsions of World War II devastated their hometown. Uncle Milos phoned from Prague to tell them the family flat there had been destroyed and that they should stay in the countryside. The country estate was not beyond the reach of the bombings, either. Václav witnessed the fallout firsthand. In a gesture that would become characteristic of his reaction to difficult situations, Václav took up his pen and described the effect the Allied attacks had on him and his family:

> On the 9th of May in the morning Zd'arec was bombed because German troops who had not surrendered were still there. After the air raid many residents of Zd'arec came to our house to seek shelter. In the afternoon, we experienced a stampede of German troops near us and shooting at them . . . Russian shells almost landed on Havlov . . . we children were afraid (and I think the grown-ups were as well). At that moment I wanted to be in Australia and little Ivan pooed himself.

Havel's record of the bombings is revealing of the artist and leader he would become as an adult: unflappable, honest, empathetic, realistic, ironic, and funny.

The Allied bombings did not last very long, though hundreds in Prague were killed. The Germans soon fled and Soviet tanks rolled into Prague in May of 1945. Initially, the Soviets were seen as liberators and were greeted with flowers and cheers. The celebration did not last long, however.

The United States, Britain, and the Soviet Union had joined forces against Hitler's Germany. But the relationship between the democratic and capitalist United States and Britain, and the totalitarian communist Soviet Union was always tense. Before the war they had been enemies, each side advocating radically different ideas of how society and economies should be operated. Not long after the war ended, the old tensions returned. Only this

time the world had been introduced to nuclear weapons and the Soviet Union was more determined than ever to expand its sphere of influence. This was the beginning of a decades-long conflict that came to be called the Cold War.

The leader of the Soviet Union in 1945 was Joseph Stalin. Stalin had come to power after the death of Vladimir Lenin, who had led the revolution that overthrew the Russian czarist government in 1917. Stalin had come to power in the late 1920s and had consolidated his grip on Soviet society in a series of bloody purges throughout the 1930s. Stalin killed anyone he thought rivaled his power. He also instituted economic changes that forced millions of people from their homes and farms and into state-run factories and agricultural communes. Stalin was determined to rapidly transform his nation from a state based on private property to one that met the Communist ideas of the German philosopher Karl Marx.

Marx's goal was to end what he saw as exploitation of the working class by capitalists, those who owned the lands, factories, and other businesses, by giving power to the "proletariat," or urban workers. In Marx's utopian vision there would be no rich and poor, powerful and powerless. Everyone would work to the best of his or her ability and receive everything they needed for a full and satisfying life. It was an idea that appealed to millions during the last decades of the nineteenth and the early twentieth century. This was the era of rapid industrialization, when a very few amassed great wealth and a much larger number worked in horrible conditions for subsistence wages.

Marx predicted that the conditions of early capitalism would grow so terrible that it would become unbearable. Then, under the guidance of a group of enlightened revolutionaries, the workers would rise up and overthrow the exploitive capitalist system. Then a Socialist state would develop, in which the distribution of wealth and goods would be determined by an enlightened leadership and would be based on need, not on competition or market forces. Eventually, this Socialist state would give way to an ideal Communist society, in which the equal separation of goods would work so smoothly that much of the state apparatus necessary in the Socialist phase would wither away. Marx predicted that what he had anticipated was unavoidable. It would be the result of inevitable historical forces.

In practice, however, the implementation of Marx's ideas in Russia and other states turned out to be far from utopian. The theory of communism was assumed to be infallible. The result was a state that was highly oppressive, overwhelmingly bureaucratic, and inflexible.

Such a radical societal change did not happen naturally, after all. It had to be effected by a dedicated, even fanatical core of people. This ironically created a separate class of society, the party leaders, who worked to reshape society and economy. Communist leaders, such

Philospher, economist, and revolutionary, Karl Marx. (Library of Congress)

as Stalin, insisted on having total control of all aspects of society and ruthlessly purged anyone, or any group, they thought stood in the way of their plans. The destruction of the old order often meant devastating important elements of society. Multiparty parliamentary democracy was replaced with a one-party state. All private property was to be "collectivized" and the state took control of institutions, including schools, theaters and the press. Many of the most talented and those skilled at running businesses and other institutions were killed or fled into exile.

In order to ensure that everyone was following the path to communism, there was strict ideological control placed on all areas of life, especially culture and education. In schools, for example, only Socialist literature, art, or philosophy could be taught. Although Marx predicted equality, the Soviet Union was a top-down society in which everything was rigidly controlled and everyone was forced to follow the dictates of the Communist Party, rather than their own will or conscience.

Stalin ruled the Soviet Union by fear. He presided over an elaborate system of secret police, gulags (concentration camps), and methodical purges in which thousands upon thousands of Soviets were denounced as traitors to the ideology of communism. Stalin was determined to make the Soviet Union into a great world power. That meant changing his vast land from a predominantly agricultural economy to one based on industry. Millions of people were relocated to make his dream come true.

At the war's end, Stalin's Red Army occupied Czechoslovakia as well as most of Eastern Europe. As the people of Czechoslovakia soon discovered, Stalin had no intention of bringing the Red Army home. He was determined to install Soviet-style communism in all the lands occupied by his mighty army. The citizens of Czechoslovakia soon discovered they had exchanged one system of totalitarian domination for another.

This reality was made clear to the Havels fairly quickly. Uncle Milos was informed in June 1945 that he was considered to be of dubious character. Milos was harassed and imprisoned before eventually escaping, in 1952, to West Germany. The last time Václav saw Milos was at Havlov, during Christmas of 1951. During his visit a clearly haggard Milos gave Václav and Ivan 500 crowns apiece. Milos could not stay long. Bozena feared for the safety of her boys if their association with an enemy of the state became known. Václav, now fifteen, sobbed when Milos left. Milos would live until 1968, but Václav would never see his favorite uncle again.

The immediate postwar period in Czechoslovakia was chaotic and difficult. The Communists were initially perceived as heroically anti-Nazi and made huge electoral gains after the war. In 1945-46, in an act of retribution for the German occupation, the Communists seized the property of 2.25 million German-speaking Czechoslovakians in the Sudetenland. The German residents were simply forced out of their homes. The government then turned the vacated lands over to ethnic Czechs.

The Czech Communists wisely did not seize immediate control of the government. This made the Communist influence even greater by lending party leaders a "moderate" veil of legitimacy.

In July 1947 Czechoslovakian leaders were set to embark on a trip to Paris to discuss the Marshall Plan, proposed by the United States to rebuild shattered postwar Europe. Czech Communist leaders opted out of the trip after receiving word from Joseph Stalin that the trip would break the "pact of friendship" between the Soviet Union and Czechoslovakia. Stalin did not want Czechoslovakia to accept U.S. aid. This desire to not participate in the Marshall Plan effectively placed Czechoslovakia in the sphere of Soviet dominance for the next forty years.

Total Communist control came soon after. In February of 1948 the Communists held a bloodless putsch, the "Coup de Prague," seizing control of the entire government. Initially other parties were allowed to have one representative in the new Communist government. Jan Masaryk, the son and last male descendant of Czechoslovakia's first president, was kept on as foreign minister. He probably hoped to use the position to help those opposed to communism to escape. But not long after the Coup de Prague Masaryk died by falling from the window of his office. The circumstances of his death were mysterious; he left no will and his archives were carted off to Moscow almost immediately. He might have planned to go into exile himself and been murdered by the Communists to avoid the embarrassment of his fleeing from the new government. Masaryk's death was a tragic symbol. The Czech Republican era, which had been interrupted by the Nazi protectorate, was brought to a definitive end by the Communist takeover.

two

An Education in Communist Czechoslovakia

Václav Havel was forged by extremes. On one side was his educated, middle-class family, and on the other was the harsh and stark world of Eastern European communism. These forces created the predominant themes of his life and work.

The Communists considered the middle-class Havel family to be enemies of the system. They were subjected to persecution. But Havel's mother, Bozena, tried to keep her family's life as normal as possible. Her cosmopolitan ideals of education and culture led her to seek the best for her sons.

In the fall of 1947, when he was eleven years old, Václav enrolled at the King George School of Poderbrady, a private boarding school about thirty miles east of Prague. The school was founded by a man who had been a Nazi prisoner of war at Dachau. He was determined to educate a future élite that would help restore European civilization. The all-boys school had about eighty pupils, who were held to very high intellectual standards. They were taught Czech, English, Latin, and Russian. Discipline was strict and the boys were encouraged to engage in extracurricular activities, especially physical exercise such as volleyball, canoeing, bicycling, and hiking. Václav was a chubby, ungainly boy, who was neither at the top of his class academically nor particularly athletic. A classmate at the school, taking notice of Václav's shape and stature, nicknamed him *chrobak*, which in Czech means a type of cumbersome beetle. He seems to have weathered his schoolboy awkwardness fairly well. He was a solid, if not exceptional, student and made good friends at Poderbrady.

Though the family lived nearby, Václav boarded at school and got to know his classmates fairly well. Many of the eighty schoolboys would become prominent in the future. Filmmakers Milos Forman, Ivan Passer, and Jerzy Skolimowski; *Sesame Street* animator Pavel Fierlinger; Jan Skoda, the future secretary of the Czechoslovak Socialist Party; and Milan Jiricek, who would become the Czech Olympic Committee Chairman, as well as Havel's mathematician younger brother, Ivan (who invariably received higher marks than Václav), were students. Some of these classmates, like Milos Forman, would become lifelong friends, even when exile separated them for years.

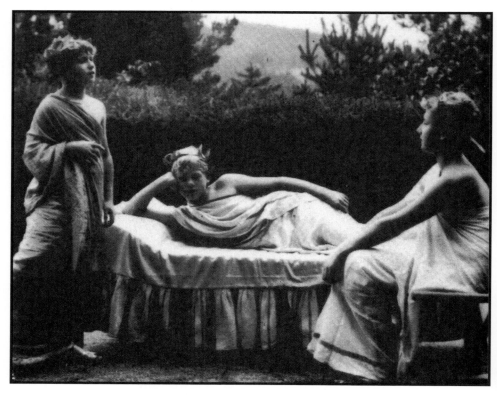

Václav's flare for the dramatic revealed itself early in life. In this photograph taken at Havlov in the summer of 1949 he poses as a Roman emperor flanked by his advisers, Ivan (left) and their friend Jan Skoda. (Havel Family Archives)

But Havel did not stay at Poderbrady long. In the spring of 1950, after only two and a half years, thirteen-year-old Václav was expelled. The reason for his expulsion was neither academic nor behavioral, but political. A secret police agent visited the school and made it clear that Václav was not an acceptable pupil. He and his family had to be taught to sacrifice for the good of communism. Václav was miserable to be separated from his classmates.

After his expulsion, Havel attended several state schools, but found the education inadequate. As Havel's friend and Poderbrady classmate Alois Strnad, who was also expelled for being a child of the bourgeoisie, reflected: "Václav simply couldn't settle down at school or take his classroom work seriously. Formal education, the target of Stalinist reforms and expulsions, resembled a bad joke." Havel also felt a keen sense of rejection and alienation at having been labeled "bourgeois," a French word that Marx had used for the middle-class capitalist who were, he said, communism's inherent enemy.

This alienation would be a theme in Havel's life, but the first stage of Havel's role as an outsider was not an act of political dissidence. It was simply childhood angst created by feeling different from his peers: "I longed for equality with others, not because I was some kind of childhood social revolutionary, but simply because I felt separate and excluded, because I felt around me a certain mistrust, a certain distance . . . I felt alone, inferior, lost, ridiculed." The persecution Havel felt made him feel ashamed of his privilege:

> Our family employed as the custom was, domestics. I had a governess; we had a cook, a maid, a gardener, and a chauffeur. All of that put, between myself and those around me (I mean my poorer fellow students and our staff) a social barrier which . . . I was very much aware of and found hard to deal with. I understood it clearly as a handicap.

Havel would later acknowledge that this early experience had a profound effect on his adult personality, "I believe this childhood experience influenced my entire future life, including my writing" he told an interviewer in 1985. "I even wonder whether the original reason I began writing, or why I try to do anything at all, was simply to overcome this fundamental experience of not belonging, of embarrassment, of fitting in nowhere, of absurdity—or rather, to learn to live with it."

The long-term benefits of Havel's experience may seem clearer in retrospect, but in the meantime, he would struggle to find his place in the new Czechoslovakia. When he was about fifteen, Václav was made a carpenter's apprentice. When he developed dizzy spells his mother worried that he would fall and hurt himself. She found her teenage son a position as an apprentice with a family friend, Otto Wichterle, a chemist and the inventor of the contact lens. At the same time, encouraged by his family, Havel took night classes to finish his secondary schooling. Havel managed to graduate, though his grades were still inferior to those of his younger brother. He applied twice for admission to Charles University in Prague and was rejected both times: by the arts faculty, then by the drama faculty because he was considered too "bourgeois" for admittance. He settled for a place at the Technical University in the economics department, studying urban transport.

Fortunately for Havel, he did not have to rely on the state to provide all of his education. As he later remembered, "I benefited from the family setting in a very direct way. I grew up in the intellectual environment of

Masarykian humanism (my father was friends with [Philosopher Emmanuel] Radl, [prominent journalist] Ferdinand Peroutka, [philosopher] J. L. Fischer, [writer] Eduard Bass, etc.): I was surrounded by good books. Intellectually I got off to a good start." Havel was intermittently tutored by his father's good friend, the Czech political philosopher J. L. Fischer. This was a very important family tie. As Havel described it, "I have fond memories of Fischer; he was the first one to raise some philosophical questions with me and draw my attention to important books of philosophy." Fischer was a highly regarded teacher. He was also an outspoken critic of Stalin, and therefore subject to harassment by the Communist government.

When he was fifteen years old—and with the active encouragement of his mother—Havel began meeting regularly with an intellectual circle that called themselves the Thirty-Sixers, after the birth year of the group's members. The circle was made up largely of disaffected bourgeois children who found life under the new Communist state intellectually stifling. It included some of Havel's fellow exiles from Poderbrady, including Honza Skoda, who first dubbed Havel *Chrobak*. The group began during a conversation between Havel and some friends who attended Prague's French Gymnasium school. A second chapter was founded in the city of Brno with the help of Jiri Paukert, who would become a close Havel associate and a famous poet.

The group coalesced around Havel, though his mother

may deserve some of the credit for that. Bozena loved seeing her son engaged as a young intellectual, and she adored his poet friend Jiri Paukert. In October of 1952 she began hosting and catering the Thirty-Sixer's meetings at the Havel's apartment in Prague. There would be around twenty such meetings in the next two years, culminating in a full-blown, weeklong retreat sponsored by Bozena at Havlov, where there were earnest philosophical discussions, poetry readings, photography shoots, and dips in the swimming pool.

The Thirty-Sixers was not just a teenage club. It was also where young Havel—though he would later recall being shy—first asserted his leadership qualities. Paukert would later say that Havel had the power to "gather around himself crowds of friends, as if he lived only to think about others and the general good." At the end of the first year of meetings, Havel wrote a twenty-eight-page assessment of the Thirty-Sixer's performance. It included ratings of individual contributions and sharp criticisms of members who merely "came, puffed on their cigarettes, and then left." Such assertiveness became characteristic of Havel.

Because the Communists had outlawed many of the group's favorite authors, including Franz Kafka, Hermann Hesse, and Karel Capek, the youngsters devoured any copies of the banned works they could get their hands on. Defying official sanctions carried great risk. Havel's insouciance in the face of power was also to become one of his chief characteristics. The Thirty-

Václav Havel in the 1950s. (Courtesy of KOTEK/AFP/Getty Images.)

Sixers probably flew under the official radar because of
their young age, but Havel later remarked how daring an
enterprise it was: "When I think back on it, my hair

stands on end: if we'd been five years older, we'd have almost certainly ended up in Mirov [the Czech labor camp]; in those days, you could easily get twenty years for that kind of thing." Havel may have been amazed in retrospect by the Thirty-Sixers' youthful indifference to danger, but he would continue to court it well into adulthood.

Life in Czechoslovakia was becoming increasingly dangerous for everyone. On July 31, 1951, Czechoslovakian President Klement Gottwald sent a telegram to Rudolph Slansky, the First Secretary of the Czechoslovak Communist Party, praising Slansky for his leadership. "You were always an effective fighter for the promulgation of the Bolshevik line against all opportunist saboteurs and traitors and for the forging of a Bolshevik party," he wrote. At the very same time 'teachers,' as Soviet advisors to Czechoslovakia were called, were busy torturing Slansky's allies into manufacturing 'evidence' that led to Slansky's disgrace and execution.

By 1951 torturing and murdering prominent party members had become a deeply ingrained characteristic of communism. Joseph Stalin had created the precedent in the Soviet Union during the 1930s. In a typical Stalin purge, party members were rounded up, tortured, and forced to read scripted "confessions" at show trials before being swiftly executed. It was an efficient way for Stalin to rid himself of enemies or potential enemies. Of course, it was all done in the name of the good of communism. Stalin's reign of terror continued throughout the 1940s and early 1950s. Men and women who never wavered in their support of Stalin were made to stand trial for crimes they had not committed. In some cases, Stalin actually had the trial's events scripted in advance, then chose the 'perpetrators' who would confess to the crimes preconceived by their accusers.

The terror fell most heavily on the leadership of the party. In Russia, many of Stalin's closest advisors were purged. In Czechoslovakia, the First Secretary was not safe. In November of 1952, while Václav Havel was suffering through the indignities of the Communist educational system, the Jewish party leader Slansky was hanged, after being accused of a wide range of crimes. Anti-Semitism was a common feature of the show trials.

Joseph Stalin's death just a few months later, in March of 1953, was a major shock to Communist Europe. Stalin's influence was so powerful that many did not believe the news at first, or continued on as though the dictator was still alive. His presence seemed to linger in the institutions he created.

Stalin's death was a turning point because it signaled a chance for reform of his terror-based state. The new leadership of the Soviet Union would temporarily disavow Stalin's legacy of murder and terror. Eventually, however, the Communist system inevitably led to more persecutions. In Czechoslovakia, Stalin's death did not even temporarily alleviate the terror. Czechoslovak party leaders feared that reforms would eventually lead to the punishment of the perpetrators of the terror, which meant they wanted to keep things the way they were. Men like Václav Kopecky, the same Minister of Information who had persecuted Havel's uncle Milos, were at the heart of this clique. While their Soviet masters attempted to bury the cult of Stalinism—new Soviet leader Nikita Khrushchev would disavow Stalin—the Czechoslovak government was still offering praise to the dictator.

The year 1956 was to prove a watershed for Eastern Europe in general and for young Václav Havel in particular. The region experienced the first tremors of anti-ommunist resistance. In neighboring Hungary, Soviet

Europe in 1955.

Hungarian citizens crowd around the vandalized head of a statue of Stalin during the revolution of 1956. (Library of Congress)

troops had to intervene to keep the government from being overthrown. Reformers rallied around Hungary's prime minister Imre Nagy and began to dismantle the Communist state. The security police headquarters were attacked, Budapest was taken over by elected councils, and when the Soviets refused to withdraw troops, Nagy announced Hungary's withdrawal from the Warsaw Pact, a military organization comprised of Communist sates, calling on the United Nations for assistance.

But help did not come. Soviet tanks entered Budapest, rolling over protesters and pitifully armed street fighters. Nagy tried to escape, but the bus ferrying him to safety was seized by Soviet troops. Nagy refused to endorse the new Soviet-installed government of János

Kádár and he was imprisoned and executed two years later. The Soviet intervention in Hungary, a bloody and merciless repression of dissent, would have a profound impact on the other members of the Warsaw Pact. It left its mark on a whole generation of Czechoslovaks.

At home, Havel found himself in an educational dead-end: "the courses did not interest me—we studied things like the nature of gravel and sand, and road construction." During his Thirty-Sixers days he had begun to frequent the Prague flat of Czech poet Vladimir Holan. Havel went to see the poet for the first time in the company of Milos Forman. There the two young men met poet Jan Zábrana, who informed them of another literary circle called Group 42, made up of prewar-era writers who had fallen out of favor under the Communist re-gime. Group 42 had been meeting regularly at the Café Slavia, the same café where Havel and his friends spent their free time, never knowing that in their midst sat the older generation of writers and intellectuals whose works inspired them. Havel tells the story of how they "discov-ered" the poet Jiri Kolár after being put on to him by Zábrana:

> My friends and I used to meet every Saturday at noon in the Café Slavia. Once Viola Fischer and I (and by the way she was the daughter of J. L. Fischer) decided to visit Kolár. We found his telephone number, and Viola, who was braver than I was, called him. He said, "Sure, come around three on Saturday." We sat in the Café Slavia, waiting impatiently, until two-thirty;

Jiri Kolár, cofounder of Group 42, would begin to branch out from traditional poetry to visual media in the 1950s. He became known for his powerful collages and development of innovative art techniques to convey the absurd, fractious character of twentieth-century Eastern Europe. (Courtesy of Tammfinearts, New Mexico.)

then we said goodbye to our friends and set out for Vrsovice to meet Kolár. When we got there, the door was opened by a gentleman who two hours before had been sitting at the table beside us in the Café Slavia and whom we knew very well by sight ... from that time—I can't remember if it was 1952 or 1953— until the 1960s, various friends of my own age and I would sit with Kolár at his famous table in the Café Slavia.

The effect of getting involved with Kolár and his Group 42 associates would be profound for Havel:

> These sessions in Kolár's circle opened up to me hitherto unknown horizons of modern art. But, most important of all, they were a kind of university of writers' morality, if I may put it in such august terms. Kolár was a distinctive preacher with a great understanding for young authors and for everything new.... although later I began to write, independently of his literary influence, things that were utterly unlike what Kolár expected of me, these efforts of mine, both in literature and in the field of civic affairs, culture and politics, would be unimaginable without his initial lesson in a writer's responsibility.

Under Kolár's influence Havel sent a letter to the editors of the journal *Kveten*, which had been founded by the Czechoslovak writer's union as an organ for young writers. The writer's union was the official Communist Party agency to writers. In his letter Havel took issue with the hypocrisy of the journal's ideal of artistic expression while it submitted to the official Communist ideology. Havel felt that the editors and writers only wanted artistic expression that fell within the guidelines prescribed by the party. To Havel, this was not worthy of the name "artistic":

I wrote a letter to the editor expressing my doubts; I pointed out the internal contradictions in the magazine and its program, and I asked why it did not reflect upon the heritage of Group 42 . . . to my astonishment, *Kveten* published my letter . . . it was probably because of this, my first published text, that I found myself on a list of neophyte authors and was then officially invited to a three-day conference (or was it a political meeting?) of young writers at Dobris.

The conference at Dobris was the first time Havel tried to navigate the uneasy mixture of politics and literature. He gave a speech that picked up where his letter had left off. He said the editors of *Kveten* had been "spoiled and pampered by power from the very first lines they wrote." He criticized the journal for being the sole outlet for creative publication, the "official" organ of literary activity. How could the journal promote artistic integrity and at the same time enforce the artistic dogma of the party? He also asked questions about the nature of "Socialist" art and the journal's ignorance of the Group 42 writers who were such an important influence for him. This critique won him cheers, especially from the older members of the crowd, who had long struggled with censorship.

Others defended the journal. His speech sent the conference into a frenzy of debate, with many in attendance unsure how to react. In Havel's view, "this confusion reflected something of the general confusion of that whole era: Stalin had fallen from grace; Hungary was bleeding in revolution . . . and no one knew where it was all heading, what still applied and what no longer did, and what one should think at all."

A gauntlet had been thrown down in the Czechoslovak literary world. A dissident voice had been heard for the first time. As Havel recognized, "my entry into public life, then, had a whiff of rebellion about it, and this has somehow clung to me: many still consider me a controversial person, to this day. Not that I welcome it: I am certainly not a revolutionary . . . it just seems that, given the logic of things, I always manage to find myself, whether I want to or not, in such a position." Havel may have been reluctant to recognize it, but he was about to embark on one of the most daringly revolutionary literary and political careers of the twentieth century.

three
A PLAYWRIGHT
IS BORN

While hanging around the Café Slavia Václav Havel met Olga Splichalová, a young woman who shared his passion for literature, politics, and, above all, theater. Olga was beautiful and highly intelligent. She loved art history and literature, and was adapting Jane Austen's *Pride and Prejudice* for a Czech Television script. Olga was also a very tough young woman. Born in the Zizkov district of Prague, the roughest working-class neighborhood in the city, Olga combined her street smarts with an incredibly lucid view of politics. She was raised by her mother, a dedicated supporter of the Communist regime, but Olga openly scorned the Communists, even as a teenager. Three years older than Havel, she loved his way with words, and he loved her fiery spirit and no-nonsense view of the world.

Havel and Olga at the Café Slavia in 1958. (Havel Family Archives)

Havel had given up on his studies at the technical university and in 1957, disaffected with his cushy but unsatisfying post as lab assistant, he resigned, making himself eligible for the draft. At the same time he was discovering love, as well as his taste for politics and literature at the Dobris conference, Havel also began his compulsory service in the Czechoslovak army. He served with the motorized artillery division at Ceské Budejovice, south of Prague. He was enrolled for a two-year stint in the army and assigned to the sappers, the corps in the army in charge of placing, removing, and otherwise dealing with mines, charges, and other explosives. According to Havel, "I served with the sappers in Ceské Budejovice and had a rather hard time of it. They probably put me with the sappers because of my social origins: our army borrowed from the Soviets the tradition of sending the less worthwhile elements of the population to serve with the sappers, because in any action the sappers go in first and lose a higher percentage of men."

Army life may have been hard on Havel, but it also provided him the opportunity to put on his first theatrical production. He and a friend from his regiment, Karel Brynda, who would later become head of drama at the State Theater in Ostrava, decided to put on a version of Czech playwright Pavel Kohout's *September Nights*. Havel played the role of Lieutenant Skrovanek, an ambitious type who covets the position of his superior, a dim-witted ideologue in charge of political affairs. Havel's performance proved too convincing, however, as his company commander missed the humor, took the play literally, and accused Havel of having designs on his job. Havel was punished but as he noted later, it was "in a way that I welcomed: he demoted me from *pancerovinik* [a position in the Czech army], which he considered an honor, and in doing so he liberated me from the responsibility of dragging a bazooka, along with everything else I had to carry, to every drill, and cleaning it every Saturday."

Using the extra time he had put into polishing his bazooka, Havel managed to put together an original script with Brynda that they planned to put on at the all-army theater festival in Mariánské Lázne, a town on the

Sergeant Ivan Havel and Private Václav Havel (right), *1959.* (Havel Family Archives)

German border. The play, *The Life Ahead*, was about an army private, Pavel Marsik. Marsik falls asleep on guard duty and wakes up to the sound of gunfire and finds a dead body. Marsik realizes the man has been shot with his rifle, taken accidentally by the officer on duty while Marsik was asleep. The intruder turns out to be a civilian, so Marsik and the officer have to concoct an alibi. The ruse works all too well; Marsik gets credited with performing a heroic act, then gets promoted and written up in the paper. He is asked to join the Communist Party. He accepts, but then falters, unable to continue the lie during his induction speech, bringing about his disgrace. The play was a great success with Havel's regiment, but not with his commanders. As Havel describes it:

> When the time came to take the play to the all-army festival in Mariánské Lázne, and there was a danger that we might actually win, the main political administration of the army took a close look at our personnel files and came, quite properly, to the conclusion that we were making fun of them. ... In the end, we did go to Mariánské Lázne, and we even performed the play, though not as part of the competition, merely so that we could be properly exposed for what we were. The next day, a large tribunal of sorts was held, and our play was condemned as antiarmy. An analysis of the play presented by one of the lieutenants (we later became friends; he turned into a reform communist and was constantly apologizing to me for that incident) argued, for instance,

that the play did not sufficiently exalt the role of the regimental party organization, or that it was unthinkable for a Czechoslovak soldier to fall asleep while on guard duty. We found it all very funny, and we were glad to be able to spend a week in Marianske Lazne with no regular army duties.

Many of the themes that Havel would develop as a mature playwright were present in *The Life Ahead*: a tortuous, bureaucratic world, a poor slob caught up in the works, a vague notion of threatened violence, and a pervasive and absurd sense of powerlessness. At the time, the only acceptable style of literature in Czechoslovakia was socialist realism, the official party style. Theater was to concentrate only on spreading the Marxist-Leninist dogma or on disparaging the bourgeois past that came before it. All socialist realist plays ended in a harmonious resolution brought about by the wise application of Marxist-Leninist ideology. Havel's plays, from the very beginning, displayed none of this.

In Havel's work there are no obvious heroes, as his characters are all in sorry shape and deteriorating fast. There is very little moralizing, and no propaganda. Havel does not want his audience to bond with the play, to be absorbed into the action. The absurdity of the situation forces the viewer to engage in the construction of meaning, rather than receiving it as assumed knowledge. Havel's defiance of party dogma was a major part of his work and, though he was able to express his disagreement with official ideology for a time through the theater, his plays would eventually create conflict with the regime.

When Havel's undistinguished career in the military came to an end, without further incident, he had no idea what to do next: "I wasn't really anything and I had no idea what I was going to do. I couldn't get into any humanities courses . . . and my efforts to study at the technical university had come to nothing too. I didn't know whether to look for work in a factory, or to try to find a job that was closer to my own interests." Fortunately for Havel, his own interests were shared by a friend of the family. Jan Werich was a playwright, performer, entertainer, and friend of Havel's father. Werich ran the ABC Theater in Prague and he hired Havel as a stagehand in 1959. It was exactly the foot in the door the young Havel needed. The ABC experience would help to develop Havel's view of the theater as a locus of freedom, a place where the programmed world of socialist realism was already being defied:

> The season I worked at the ABC was decisive. By sheer coincidence it was Werich's last season in the theater. Under Werich, the ABC Theater was a dying echo of the old Liberated Theater, and I was fortunate enough to be able to breathe, literally at the last minute, something of its atmosphere. It was there I came to understand—because I could observe it daily from the inside—that theater doesn't have to be just a factory for the production of plays or, if you like, a

mechanical sum of its plays, directors, actors, ticket-sellers, auditoriums, and audiences; it must be something more: a living spiritual and intellectual focus, a place for social self-awareness, a vanishing point where all the lines of force of the age meet, a seismograph of the times, a space, an area of freedom, an instrument of human liberation. I realized that every performance can be a living and unrepeatable social event, transcending in far-reaching ways what seems, at first sight, to be its significance.

Havel pitched in with every aspect of production at the theater while also developing his own dramatic oeuvre. He wrote articles on dramatic theory for a magazine called *Divadlo*, and collaborated on a script, which, though never performed, was good enough to land him a job in the summer of 1960 at Prague's Theater on the Balustrade.

The Balustrade was part of a renaissance of small theaters in Prague, where only large state-run theaters had thrived since the war. The ABC had helped to keep the spirit of the small, pre-war, independent theater alive. Now others were picking up that thread to the past and expanding on it. The excitement generated by this was palpable to Havel, who felt that, "no matter how the performance turned out, one thing was certain: it was full of the joy of performance, there was freedom, pure humor, and intelligence in it; it didn't take itself too seriously, and people were delighted. In short, something new and unprecedented was born."

Prague's Theater on the Balustrade, where Havel produced his first play, is still an operating theater today.

The concurrence of elements that made Havel so excited—young, talented, creative people, a tie to the pre-Communist past, and small-scale productions that allowed for a wide range of artistic freedom and relatively little notice from the authorities—made the theater in Prague an island of relative freedom in communist Czechoslovakia.

In collaboration with Ivan Vyskocil, the dramatic director of the Balustrade, Havel produced his first play. *Hitchhiking,* produced in 1961, was a satire of Socialist society. Officially, Communists were not supposed to covet material goods the way people in capitalist societies did. Havel played with the fact that materialism did not disappear under communism; rather, it merely found alternative means of expression.

Havel was completely immersed in the Balustrade. He performed a variety of tasks, from stagehand to dramaturge, "but, it didn't really matter which of those jobs I held in any given moment, and often I held them concurrently: in the morning I organized tours, in the evening I ran the lighting for the performance, and at night I rewrote plays." Havel would later say, "that period was extremely important for me, not only because those eight years in the Theater on the Balustrade were in fact the only period when I was able to devote myself fully to theater, to the only kind of theater that interested me, but also because it formed me as a playwright."

His first solo production at the Balustrade was in 1964. The play, *The Garden Party,* tells the story of good-for-nothing Hugo Pludek, who gets pushed by his ambitious father to attend a garden party put on by a strange bureaucratic department called the Liquidation Office. Hugo is there in order to meet an acquaintance of his father's who is a higher-up in the department. The official never shows up, but Hugo winds up rising to power in the Liquidation Office by exploiting a rift with the rival Inauguration Office, whose representative is in attendance to inaugurate the Liquidation Office Garden Party. Hugo succeeds because he is a conformist, molding himself to whatever those around him want to see or hear, all the while spouting nonsensical truisms he learned from his blindly ambitious but inept father: "The point is that today we need action, not words! One should never fire a blunderbuss into the nettles."

In direct contradiction to Hugo's call to action, the drama presents nothing but words; in fact, the whole play is almost entirely devoid of action. Hugo's words prove that he has lost practically all capacity for meaningful communication. Bureaucratic terminology is repeated mechanically by the characters until it reaches a climax when Hugo returns home and his parents do not recognize him. They ask who he is and Hugo's response is a full-scale exercise in absurdity:

> Me! You mean who I am? Now look here, I don't like this one-sided way of putting questions, I really don't. . . . today the time of static and unchangeable categories is past, the time when A was only A, and B always only B is gone; today we all know very well that A may be often B as well as A; that B may just as well be A; that B may be B, but equally it may be A and C; just as C may be not only C, but also A, B, and D; and in certain circumstances even F may become Q, Y, and perhaps also H.

The Garden Party was Havel's response to the forced compliance of communism. In order to make itself the sole proprietor of truth, the Communist Party was obliged to make everyone comply with official ideology. In the Communist bureaucracy, it was the most readily compliant individual, not the most talented, who got ahead. But that person would then have to be dubbed the most talented in order to justify his or her promotion. Havel's play pokes fun at the hypocritical and inefficient system. It has since been described as unperformable because of the absurdist dialogue and lack of plot.

Havel's mother was not pleased by his choice of career—which at the time meant abandoning his formal education—or with his relationship with Olga. Unlike his mother, Olga supported Havel's decision to pursue drama. Olga was serious about their relationship, taking a night job as an usher at the Balustrade so they could spend their days together. When he accepted her offer of marriage, they were wed in a no-frills civil ceremony on July 9 of 1964 in the town hall of Zizkov, the rough neighborhood of Olga's youth. Havel—who was only seventeen when they met—was now twenty-eight. Olga was thirty-one. They went out to lunch after the ceremony to celebrate with Jan Grossman, their boss and official witness to the marriage, then went to work that night at the Balustrade. Their marriage would last for four decades, through both personal and professional ups and downs.

four

PTYDEPE

During the decade of the 1960s the relationship between the Communist Bloc and the capitalist countries in the West gradually changed. The Communist Bloc was composed of all the nations on the Soviet side of the "Iron Curtain," which came to be symbolized by the giant wall the East German Communists built to divide East Berlin from West Berlin. Essentially, this was a formalization of the military situation that had existed when World War II ended and Europe was divided between pro-Western and pro-Communist nations.

The Cold War between communism and capitalism reached its intensity in the early 1960s. The Berlin Wall was built in 1961 because relations had soured to the point the East Germans decided to seal its border to keep its citizens from fleeing to the West. The countries to the west of the Iron Curtain joined the North Atlantic Treaty Organization, or NATO. Those in the Soviet sphere were drawn into the Warsaw Pact.

After the climactic Cuban Missile Crisis, in which the U.S. and the Soviet Union almost went to war over the placement of Soviet nuclear missiles in Communist Cuba in 1962, the two sides began to look for ways to avoid total war. Conditions remained tense, but much of the conflict took place in less strategic locations, such as the long war in Southeast Asia. By the 1970s the Soviet leaders and the West had entered into a phase they called détente—not reconciliation but an increasing willingness to accept each side's existence.

The 1960s were a decade of change within many other countries as well. The United States was increasingly occupied with the Civil Rights Movement, which finally began to address the racial inequalities left over from the Civil War of a hundred years earlier. By the end of the decade the country was almost paralyzed by a debate over the U.S.-led war against Communist insurgences in Vietnam and other parts of Southeast Asia. This combination of factors led to the emergence into the mainstream of a youth-inspired counterculture that began to question many of the policies, ideals, and verities of earlier generations.

These societal changes were naturally slower to develop in the tightly controlled Communist Bloc. Stalin had pressured Czechoslovakia to reject the Marshall Plan and accept Soviet "friendship" instead. The countries that rejected help from the West were joined together in the Warsaw Pact agreement of mutual assistance and friendship. These countries included Czechoslovakia as well as Hungary, Bulgaria, Romania, Poland, Albania, Austria, and East Germany—all places where the Communist Party had taken total control.

After the purges of the 1950s, Czechoslovakia was led by Antonin Novotny, who held the post of First Secretary of the Communist Party and President of Czechoslovakia. Novotny led the Presidium, the supreme leadership council of the party. It presided over

President of Czechoslovakia from 1957 to 1968, Antonin Novotny oversaw the replacement of the Czechoslovakian democracy by a one-party communist state.
(Library of Congress)

750 *aparatchiks*, or central party officials, who in turn oversaw some 8,500 employees of the national party administration. Beyond this central authority were the 300,000 members of various party committees on local levels. Then there was the general party membership, which fluctuated, but at some points neared one million, out of twelve million citizens. Ironically, the Communist system, which in theory should have leveled society, was very hierarchical. The closer one was to the central party apparatus, the more influence, power, and privilege was available. The central party administration held a virtual monopoly on luxury goods, quality housing, vacations, and other comforts.

In the early sixties this system began to experience some crises. It was not simply a matter of power or privilege creating resentment. The fundamental problem was that the top-down, demand-driven system was inefficient and unable to meet the basic needs of its people. All decisions on trade, production, supply, and consumption were left to the state. By the mid-1960s the governing Presidium could no longer handle even the most basic day-to-day decisions. Power was concentrated in too few hands, and those who held it were often not up to the task.

In the West people were helped through bad economic times by aspects of what is often called "civil society," a broad term used to describe all sorts of non-governmental organizations: charities, clubs, churches, trade unions, civic groups, even informal circles of friends and associates, such as Havel's Thirty-Sixers. But almost all of the private groups that might have intervened to make the economic downturn more bearable for the populace had been eradicated by the Communist regime.

The Czechoslovak people began to grow frustrated. The frustration simmered beneath the surface at first, but eventually boiled over. Voices from all sectors of society called for a liberalization of the regime. Alexander Dubcek, who would soon become the reformist First Secretary of the Communist Party, would later reflect that the hard-liners in the regime had "failed again in their attempts to silence the opposition, especially in Slovakia. Discontent was growing . . . we learned from reports of the district party committees that the public mood in both Slovakia and the Czech lands was increasingly impatient and in favor of change."

In Dubcek's native Slovakia there was open discontent because the Communist system had failed to address the ongoing problem of the under-representation of Slovaks in state institutions. In the universities, students voiced dissatisfaction with dormitory conditions—which were shabby and crowded—as well as restrictions on studying abroad and boring required courses on Marxism and Leninism. In the arts, where the trend was shifting from the large official state institutions to smaller, more experimental establishments, like the ABC or the Balustrade Theaters, continued pressure for innovation and liberalization was mounting.

Havel would play a part in the fight for liberalization within the writers' community. It began while he served on the editorial board of the journal *Tvár (The Face)*. He had not previously been a member of the Writers' Union. He was busy with his own work, and was estranged from the "official" cultural organ of the party. When the union founded *Tvár* as an outlet for young writers, as *Kveten* had been before it, Havel initially had a low opinion of the journal: "to tell you the truth, I felt a certain inner distance from that whole group . . . while

I was being a lab assistant or building pontoon bridges or working as a stagehand, unable to get into any school . . . these fellows . . . went straight into jobs with publishing houses and magazines." However, in 1965 a new group took over the *Tvár* editorial board. Havel was in agreement with their vision: "their aims appealed to me in every way, and in fact were close to mine," he said later.

Havel knew that the new board had ulterior motives when they asked him to join. Because they had not published, none was eligible to be a member of the Writers' Union and could not defend the journal at union meetings. Havel was eligible for membership in the Union. When he agreed to join *Tvár*, he was also agreeing to join the Writers' Union. Under Havel, *Tvár* would become the locus of the most daring and experimental material in the Czechoslovak literary world.

The Writers' Union was at that time controlled by reform Communists, who were pushing for "liberalization" within the Communist regime. The reformers wanted change, but still remained loyal to certain party principles. Even for the reformists, *Tvár* was radical because it did not publish party-approved material. Instead, Havel and his friends used *Tvár* to publish authors outside the Communist ideological realm. As Havel put it, *Tvár* was a "an island of freedom in an ocean of something that thought of itself as immensely free but in fact was not." What's more, in almost every issue of *Tvár*, reviewers tore one of the best sellers of the period to shreds. Many of the savaged books were written by Writers' Union members.

This situation inevitably led to trouble. Havel was soon called upon to defend *Tvár*. He did so at a conference of the Writers' Union in 1965, giving a speech in which he criticized the Union for its bureaucracy, inflexibility, and intolerance of the many authors excluded from membership. Exclusion from the party's graces meant that a writer could not publish or be employed by a publishing house; he or she was excluded from the business of literature altogether. Havel's speech was greeted with thunderous applause by the very people he was criticizing.

Havel managed to keep *Tvár* alive for a time, but eventually the Union's Central Committee was pressured by the Communist Party to ban the journal. Havel and his friends circulated a petition protesting the decision that gathered about two hundred signatures. They then started another petition, this time demanding that the Writers' Union meet expressly to decide the fate of the journal. When it became clear that they might actually succeed in getting enough signatures to force a meeting the party intervened, pressuring writers not to sign. Pavel Auersperg, head of the Cultural Department of the Communist Party, the government agency which oversaw the Writers' Union and all official state cultural outlets, even offered Havel a bribe: his own magazine, with editorial rights to commission work from the board of *Tvár*.

Václav (far right) *with his family in the 1960s.* From left to right: *his brother Ivan, his wife Olga, his father and his mother.* (Courtesy of KOTEK/AFP/Getty Images.)

Havel refused the bribe, and though they fell short of the required signatures to call a meeting, he felt he had learned an important lesson: "don't get mixed up in back-room wheeling and dealing, but play an open game." However, Havel later did not always avoid "back-room wheeling and dealing."

The *Tvár* controversy was Havel's first engagement in a political struggle. Before, Havel had been, according to his own description, "someone who lived only for his work in the theater, and was no more than a curious observer of anything beyond that. Thanks to *Tvár*, I stepped outside this circle, without really knowing where the inner logic of the step would take me." As Havel put it, "it was . . . the beginning of my 'rebellious' involvement with the Writers' Union . . . at the same time, it was the beginning of something deeper—my involvement in cultural and civic politics—and it ultimately led to my becoming a 'dissident.'"

After *Tvár* was shut down, Havel and his friends organized a wake that was actually more of an extensive pub-crawl through Prague. It was December, and while staggering home, they came upon a pile of freshly cut Christmas trees. The revelers each helped themselves to a tree, but were stopped by a policeman, who asked to see receipts. Instead, one of them pulled out a press pass. The officer, taken by surprise, and clearly wanting to avoid showing up in the papers, looked at the pass and replied: "You mind your business, we'll mind ours!"

After the *Tvár* fight, Havel did not rush to take on the

party directly. However, he could not restrain himself when the party claimed *Tvár* had been closed to make it better. Havel could not stand this type of doublespeak and hypocrisy. In response, he wrote one of his most memorable plays, *The Memorandum*.

The Memorandum tells the story of Josef Gross, the managing director of a department in an undefined, bleak bureaucracy. Gross comes to work one day to find a memorandum on his desk written in a strange, garbled language. To his dismay, he finds that everyone else in the office is already aware of the new language's existence.

Ptydepe, as it's known, is an artificial language developed to avoid the messy complications of normal human language. Words are purposefully constructed so as not to be similar to one another: 60 percent of the letters in any word must be different from those in any other word of the same length, and the more common a word is, the shorter. So, for example, the word for 'wombat' has 319 letters, but the word for "whatever," a perfect expression for use in a nonsensical bureaucracy, is spelled simply "gh." Gross also discovers that his deputy, Ballas, is responsible for the introduction of *Ptydepe* and seems to be plotting against him. Ballas tells Gross the memorandum is likely a performance review resulting from Gross's misuse of a company stamp. Gross winds up as Ballas's deputy in a bizarre coup, unable to confront the *Ptydepe* phenomenon because he finds himself utterly unable to communicate.

For example, when he goes to the translation department—the only ones who seem to be able to understand the new language—to have his memo rendered into natural language, the following exchange occurs between the character Gross and the translation department employees Helena, Savant, and Stroll:

> GROSS: What can a staff member do in such a case?
> HELENA: He can have his memo translated. Listen everybody! Today your coffee's hyp nagyp! (MARIA passes cups to STROLL, SAVANT, and HELENA, then takes the iron and runs out through the side door.)
> SAVANT: Nagyp avalyx?
> HELENA: Nagyp hayfazut! (STROLL, SAVANT, and HELENA pass the spoon around, offer sugar to each other, sip their coffee with gusto, absorbed in their Ptydepe conversation. GROSS, growing more and more desperate, turns from one to the other.)
> GROSS: Mr. Stroll—
> STROLL: Hayfazut gyp andaxe. (to GROSS) Yes?
> SAVANT: Andaxe bel jok andaxu zep?
> GROSS: In order to make a translation from Ptydepe, you require an authorization from Dr. Savant—
> HELENA: Andazu zep.
> STROLL: Ejch tut zep. Notut?
> GROSS: Dr. Savant—
> SAVANT: Tut. Gavych ejch lagorax. (to GROSS) Yes?
> HELENA: Lagorax hagyp.
> GROSS: In order to grant the authorization, you require the documents from Miss Helena—

STROLL: Lagorys nabarof dy Zoro Bridel caf o abagan.
SAVANT: Mavolde gyzot abagan?
GROSS: Miss Helena—
HELENA: Abaan Fajfor! (to GROSS) Yes?
STROLL: Fajfor? Nu rachaj?
GROSS: In order to issue the documents, you require that a staff member have his memorandum translated—
SAVANT: Rachaj gun.
HELENA: Gun Snojvep?
STROLL: Znojvep yj.
SAVANT: Yj rachaj?

The upshot of this frustrating conversation is that there is no way to have the memo translated, because no one in the organization—except for one person who was subsequently transferred to steamship navigation—has managed to figure the language out. They are all just pretending. Even Ballas, the very deputy whose idea *Ptydepe* was, has no idea how to speak or read it.

What's more, the language has shown signs of developing the very emotional ambiguities it was designed to avoid as soon as it is used by human beings. The entire drama of the first act is seemingly resolved when *Ptydepe* is eliminated and Gross is returned to his post as Managing Director. But Ballas persists; first, he refuses Gross's order to leave the department. Then, in an absurd recurrence of the first act, Ballas introduces another artificial language, *Chorukor*, supposedly an improvement on *Ptydepe*. Gross is outraged but he is also trapped.

Though he is, as he says, "attempting to salvage the last remnants of Man's humanity," he has few ways to achieve that goal. Gross is a classic Havelian character, confused and caught up in the frustration of living in an unfeeling, bureaucratic world.

five

PRAGUE SPRING

Absurdist satire, like *The Memorandum*, may have been one of the only ways to respond to Communist oppression. The play was produced in 1965, just as the twenty-nine-year-old Havel was becoming politically active for the first time. The next few years saw a continued progress of the "antidogmatists" in the party, and the resulting thaw allowed Havel to travel abroad.

In the spring of 1968 *The Memorandum* opened in New York. Václav and Olga flew in for opening night. However, during a layover in Paris, the Havels delayed at the airport in order to meet Pavel Tigrid, a Czech writer living in exile, and were caught in what was probably the largest strike in French history. The mass strike was led by the younger generation, rebelling against what they saw as an archaic, repressive system. Hundreds of thousands—perhaps as many as a million—demonstrators filled the streets. Schools were closed, transport came to a halt as the May Days of 1968 were in full swing. Then, when they finally managed to fly on to America, the Havels landed in the middle of one of the most turbulent years in U.S. history.

The U.S. was wracked by political and cultural changes in 1968. The Vietnam War was dragging on and there had developed a protest movement against it. Martin Luther King Jr. and Robert Kennedy were assassinated within a few weeks of each other. Some thought the country was coming apart. Havel witnessed the climate created by these events, and it impacted him profoundly. Not only did it reinforce his burgeoning sense of artistic resistance and expression, but he went back to Prague literally adorned with the "spirit of '68": wearing a peace medallion he had purchased in New York. His travels abroad reinforced Havel's belief in the importance of artistic freedom.

In spite of the tumultuous world climate, the late 1960s was a time of relative peace and tranquility for the Havels personally. In 1967 Václav and Olga found a house and some land in the village of Hrádecek, northeast of Prague, on the Polish border. Though Havel always referred to it as his "cottage," it was actually more of a country estate, or small castle. In the summer of 1968 they hosted parties for friends who came in droves. Havel seemed to be trying to recreate the wild atmosphere of freedom he had experienced abroad. He played rock music brought back from America and cooked experimental dishes. Some guests stayed for days, weeks, or even the whole summer.

The revelry took place after a dramatic change in the Czechoslovak Communist Party. In 1968 Alexander Dubcek was elected First Secretary of the party. Dubcek, a Slovak not known for his great leadership skills, was chosen because Antonin Novotny, the outgoing First Secretary, thought that nominating him would allow him to reconsolidate his hold on power. He did not think Dubcek was up for the job.

Novotny's plan backfired. Dubcek's reign as First Secretary led to a dramatic opening of Czechoslovak society. The May Day parade—which in Communist countries is the celebration of International Workers' Day—held in Prague in 1968 was a rapturous occasion. It was hailed as the "spring of our new existence" in the press. It really seemed as though a new world had been created in a single springtime, though as Havel put it later, "I understand 1968 as the logical outcome and culmination of a long process, lasting for many years, in which, as I say, society gradually became aware of itself and liberated itself."

Whatever the origins of the reforms, society was changing. There was greater freedom of the press, people began to speak openly of subjects that had been taboo for years, and associations flourished that had been previously unthinkable. The phenomenon would come to be known as the Prague Spring. Havel was euphoric:

"Just think of it. Suddenly you could breathe freely, people could associate freely, fear vanished, taboos were swept away, social conflicts could be openly named and described, a wide variety of interests could be expressed, the mass media once again began to do their proper job, civic self-confidence grew: in short, the ice began to melt."

Havel met Dubcek when he was invited to a state dinner in early July 1968. He seized the opportunity— buoyed by generous portions of Cognac—to share his views on several matters with Dubcek: "I advised him to allow the Social Democrats [a Leftist party more moderate than the Communists] to come back and not to cause difficulties for the former political prisoners. . . . I told him he should get rid of any illusions about the Kremlin, that he shouldn't always be on the defensive and trying to pacify public opinion . . . of course, he didn't follow much of my advice, but the fact that he talked to me at all won me over."

Despite the excitement, Havel had concerns about the Prague Spring; he saw many reasons to worry. There may have been reform, but the leaders of the reform were the same Communist ideologues who had been running things for years. They lacked perspective and vision and had been so indoctrinated by Communist ideology that they could not see beyond the system. Even Alexander Dubcek, who became emblematic of the reform

Opposite: A relaxed-looking Havel cooks in the kitchen at Hrádecek during the heady days of the late 1960s. (Courtesy of Getty Images.)

Communists of the Prague Spring era, said, "I did not see why the concept [of a centralized state economy] should not work, because then I had almost unlimited confidence in centralized economic planning, thinking the flaws of the system were mainly caused by poor management. All that was needed, I thought, was to make it more ingenious and flexible." He would add that "only over time did I come to realize that the problem was the system itself . . . it needed to be dismantled."

As the reform Communists implemented limited changes—easing restrictions on travel, scaling back censorship, allowing greater freedom of assembly, and permitting political associations other than the party— the party reformers began to be overwhelmed.

Dubcek and his allies were trying to institute what they called "socialism with a human face," a system that would eliminate the totalitarian excesses of the previous regime but maintain a state-run economy. The so-called Action Program, brought out in April 1968, was indicative of the schizophrenic nature of what they were attempting. The Action Program flattered the Soviets while at the same time encouraging reforms bound to bring Czechoslovakia into conflict with the Kremlin. The reformers failed to anticipate the Soviet response.

In July 1968 the Soviet Union began a series of military maneuvers with other Warsaw Pact troops on Czechoslovak territory. The message was clear. Dubcek and other Czech leaders met with the Soviet leaders to discuss the matter. The discussions took place, starting on July 29, in the Czech border town of Cierna. The Soviets, led by Premier Leonid Brezhnev, arrived each morning in a train with bulletproof windows and each night retreated three hundred yards back to Soviet territory. This was symbolic of the Soviet attitude: they came to dictate terms and then go home. They were not interested in negotiating in good faith. The two sides signed an "agreement" in Bratislava at the end of the talks that stated the intention of continued cooperation between the two nations, but the crisis was far from resolved.

On August 10, the Dubcek government published a draft of party statutes guaranteeing, among other things, a separation of party and state power and the protection of minority opinions. This was the last straw for the Soviets. On the night of August 20-21, 1968, troops from five Communist countries—the USSR, Poland, Bulgaria, Hungary, and East Germany—supported by 7,500 tanks and a thousand planes, invaded Czechoslovakia.

The invasion of Czechoslovakia was part of a postwar pattern in Eastern Europe. The Warsaw Pact nations were allies in name only. In reality, they were subservient states to the Soviet Union. Hungary had been forced into compliance with Soviet doctrine in 1956. Poland was kept in line with almost constant Soviet saber-rattling, as were the other nations involved in the invasion. Because it promised to return power to the people, the Prague Spring was a major threat to Soviet control. If Czechoslovakia was allowed to determine its own

This iconic photograph, taken from inside a café in Prague, gives some idea of the incongruity and shock many Czechs felt at the arrival of Soviet troops in the country during the invasion following the Prague Spring. (Courtesy of Getty Images.)

course, what would stop Poland, Hungary, and the other nations from following suit? Tank columns were soon winding through the streets of Prague, while giant Antonov transport planes carrying troops landed at the Prague airport. Radio broadcasts urged the populace not to resist.

When the invasion came, Havel was close to the border, in the northern Bohemian town of Liberec. He had not been directly involved in politics during the events of the Prague Spring. He had, earlier in 1968, joined a group of fellow non-Communists in forming an institution for non-party members. The KAN Klub—or Club of Committed Non-Partisans—was, in Havel's words, "an organization with a lot of awkward problems." KAN was hastily formed, and had only vague plans, but it was "the expression of an authentic and logical social need; it was an attempt to find a solution to one of the biggest social problems of that time." In other words, the KAN Klub was an attempt to make the majority of the population—who found themselves on the outside looking in at the party—feel as though they had a voice. Later in 1968 Havel would publish a call for the creation of an opposition party in the pages of *Literárni noviny*, the leading weekly magazine of the time. But Havel would look back with skepticism on these pseudo-political efforts:

> I don't believe now that the formation of an opposition party was a realistic idea. Without the traditions, without the experiences, and without the leading personalities, it would have been just as much an exercise in futility as the KAN Klub was. Nor do I think it would have solved any essential problem. As a matter of fact, for some time now I've been skeptical about the very idea of mass political parties…but what mainly bothers me about that article now is something else. The idea of forming a new political party ought to be proposed by someone who is determined to form such a party—and I was not that person. In those

agitated times, I still saw my role as that of a writer who is simply a "witness of the time."

Havel witnessed the invading army crashing through Liberec. Soon, as Havel put it, "The Whirlwind the occupation left in its wake drew me into it."

Havel and Olga had gone to Liberec with Jan Triska to visit friends. The armies rolled through the town with great force—a tank commander at one point opened fire on an unarmed crowd—but did not occupy Liberec. After the invasion, Havel and Triska barricaded themselves in the local radio station and were given fake identification cards by local factory workers in order to conceal themselves among the workers. Local workers also ringed the station with huge transport trucks loaded with large cement blocks to prevent a takeover. Then Havel and Triska began a stint as resistance journalists. Triska read statements prepared by Havel on the radio, and the two of them appeared on a TV station they rigged up on a nearby hill.

During this week of resistance, Havel also ghost-wrote speeches for the chairman of the National Committee of the Communist Party and other party officials to be broadcast to the nation. The government, crippled by the invasion, encouraged the population to practice a kind of active ignorance of the invaders' presence. In Liberec, active resistance against the invasion flared. A youth gang called the Tramps, which had previously troubled the town with its activities, actually volunteered

Violence erupts on the streets of Prague as residents carrying a Czechoslovak flag and throwing burning torches attempt to stop a Soviet tank on August 21, 1968. (AP Photo)

for civic duty. The mayor assigned them the task of removing all the street signs to confuse the invaders. They piled them all—undamaged—outside the town hall. They then positioned themselves outside the door, checking anyone who wished to enter and protecting the mayor as his personal bodyguards. Citizens identified secret police vehicles and kept track of their movements and gave the armies wrong directions. As Havel would later recollect, "that week showed how helpless military power is when confronted by an opponent unlike any that power has been trained to confront; it showed how hard it is to govern a country in which, though it may not defend itself militarily, all the civil structures simply turn their backs on the aggressors."

Civil society, the important element of society consisting of associations, clubs, fraternal organizations, political parties, trade unions, and other groups, had only begun to reawaken in Czechoslovakia during the Prague Spring. Now the Czechoslovak people were stubbornly resisting its extinction. Havel was inspired when he saw the Tramps sitting on the Town Hall steps guarding the building and playing American pop music on their guitars. "I saw the whole thing in a special light," he reflected, "because I still had fresh memories of crowds of similar young people in the East Village in New York, singing the same song, but without the tanks in the background."

Unfortunately, those tanks would eventually make a big difference. The resistance was successful enough to convince the Soviets they had to take more drastic measures. They had successfully invaded the country and taken control, but the political situation was still unstable. On August 23 Brezhnev had the Czechoslovak leadership kidnapped and taken to Moscow. Alexander Dubcek described being taken into custody in his own office in Prague: "The main door flew open again and in walked some higher officers of the KGB . . . the little colonel quickly reeled off a list of all Czechoslovak Communist Party officials present and told us that he was taking us 'under his protection.' Indeed we were protected, sitting around that table—each one of us had a tommy gun pointed at the back of his head."

Dubcek was taken, along with Czechoslovak president Ludvik Svoboda and most of the party leadership, by armored personnel carrier to the airport. Then the whole delegation was flown to Moscow, where they were interrogated, cut off from all outside news, and refused any outside communication. For four days and nights the Soviets harangued the Czech leadership. Their demands for consultation with their country were angrily rejected. The result was that on August 26, 1968 all the Czechoslovak leaders but one—Frantisek Kriegel—signed a capitulation known as the Moscow Protocol.

Because of Kriegel's refusal to sign, the Soviets held him prisoner as the others in the delegation prepared to board their flight home. But the Czechoslovaks refused to leave without him. As Dubcek remembered, "It came up that the Soviets did not want him [Kriegel] to return with us to Prague. Brezhnev argued that the presence of the only man who did not sign the protocol could cause political difficulties. I refused to leave Kriegel behind and Svoboda supported me energetically, as did Smrkovsky, Simon, and others. Finally, Brezhnev gave in." The Soviets relented in order to avoid an incident, and the whole Czechoslovak group flew dejectedly home.

No one in the international community lifted a finger to help stave off the crushing of the Czechoslovak Prague Spring. The rest of the world may simply have been too distressed by its own upheaval to be able to respond. America was stuck in Vietnam and all over Europe student revolts and protests rocked society. Africa was shaking off colonial rule and sinking into the internecine civil conflicts that would plague the continent for the next generation. The Soviet Union was a major military power with hundreds of nuclear weapons. To stop their aggression in Czechoslovakia would risk nuclear war. These were the unspoken terms of the Cold War, hashed out during twenty years of tension between the nuclear superpowers. Czechoslovakia would have to go it alone.

six

NORMALIZATION

After returning from Moscow, Dubcek had to address his nation on the new "agreement." In a moment that became symbolic of the Soviet era, a clearly broken Dubcek told his country, in a speech punctuated by long silences and sobs, that there was reason for optimism, for foreign troops would soon be removed from Czechoslovakia. In fact, he and his colleagues had agreed to a very different arrangement. Rather than guaranteeing the withdrawal of troops, the Moscow agreement stated that the Warsaw Pact armies would withdraw only after the "anti-Socialist" element had been dealt with, which meant an open-ended occupation. It also stipulated that most of the recent reforms, such as freedom of the press and assembly, were to be curtailed. The situation in Czechoslovakia

On August 27, 1968, after his return from Moscow, Dubcek attempted to reassure his country in an emotional television address that became symbolic of the end of the Prague Spring reform movement. (Czech News Agency)

was to be "normalized"—returned to pre-1968 conditions.

Havel wrote a private letter to Dubcek encouraging him to stand fast for the sake of that nation and not lose his courage. As Havel put it, "I had written that even a purely moral act that has no hope of any immediate and visible political effect can gradually and indirectly, over time, gain in political significance." Dubcek would not heed the advice; the "purely moral" act Havel spoke of was more than he could muster. He would soon be swept from the political stage. Havel felt that by taking a stand—even a futile one—for the right principles, Dubcek could have laid the foundations for a continued struggle against Soviet tyranny. Havel would incorporate this idea into his own vision for how to lead the moral opposition to Communist rule. It would be a struggle filled with years of frustrating, seemingly ineffectual resistance to overwhelming state power, with little hope of success, but Havel would persist.

The years after the invasion were traumatic for Czechoslovakia. In January 1969, a young philosophy student named Jan Palach set himself on fire in central Prague in protest. Three more self-immolations followed in the towns of Pilsen and Brno. The events outraged the nation, but did not necessarily surprise people. As Havel observed, "Palach's death, which at any other time would have been difficult to understand, was understood immediately by the whole society, because it was an extreme and almost symbolic expression of the 'spirit of the time': everyone knew that desperate need to do something desperately extreme when everything else failed, for everyone carried such a need within himself." When asked to describe the early seventies, Havel responded: "The seventies were bland, boring, and bleak."

The "normalization" ordered by the Soviets was established formally by a law, Legislative Measure Number 99/1969, signed by Dubcek and the man who would replace him, Gustav Husák. The measure declared a permanent state of emergency, enacted serious punitive measures for anyone involved in public disturbances, extended the maximum period of detention without trial, and laid the legal groundwork for the elimination of anyone deemed undesirable in the administration, schools, theaters, academies of science, or other organizations where the Socialist order was being threatened. The measure defined a new era in Communist rule. It was to be an era of pervasive state power. The hallmark of the new state was its demand for the appearance of compliance. The government cared little what people did, so long as they kept up the appearance of being loyal citizens. Plans for reform continued, but reform now meant making the system more efficient, not changing it.

Thousands of people lost their jobs as the government reshuffled everything. Most of the ministers and all the premiers of the government were changed. The heads of the state banks and the chief prosecutors were fired, and trade unions—including the Writers' Union— were decimated and reorganized. Especially hard hit were media, culture, and entertainment.

In 1971 Havel's works were banned. Though he continued to write, he struggled. He had become a recognized playwright abroad. His work was staged in theaters from Tokyo to London, but he was forced into obscurity in his own country. He said of *The Conspirators*, the first play written after his blacklisting, "no play took me longer or was harder to write, and it's clearly the weakest of my plays." It was a very difficult time. He and Olga tried as best they could to keep in touch with friends by inviting them to Hrádecek ("our cottage") for informal congresses. The meetings were spent reading one another's texts and discussing art and literature. Apart from that, the Havels were isolated. As Havel said, "the popular term 'ghetto' seems to me the most adequate to describe the period."

Many Czechoslovaks probably felt they lived in the "ghetto." The entire society became isolated after the repression of the Prague Spring. The party had re-consolidated its control over society, taking a complete monopoly on power and decision-making. The result was a society cowed by party intimidation. No one could defy the party and hope to succeed, because the party controlled everything. It kept individuals isolated by rewarding only strict loyalty. There was not a threat of imminent death, but disagreeing with the regime meant an end to any prospects, and could result in prison time.

Havel was deeply affected. As long as he stayed in his country home, away from politics and the theater, he was left alone. But the isolation got to him. In 1974 he took a job as a laborer at the Trutnov Brewery, about six miles from Hrádecek. At the time, Havel said he needed the money, but he later admitted, "I think the real reason was that I needed a change. The suffocating inactivity all around me was beginning to get on my nerves. I wanted to get out of my shelter for a while and take a look around." What he saw could not have encouraged him. Even on an international level, the mood was not promising. During the 1970s the USSR and U.S. had entered a period called détente in which leaders from both countries agreed to reduce tensions and not to interfere in one another's affairs. Because the Communist Bloc was considered to be part of the "Soviet sphere," Western diplomats largely refrained from encouraging the dissident movement in Czechoslovakia. As Havel noted, "many of our Western friends and collaborators avoided us almost as circumspectly as official writers here did, so they wouldn't annoy the authorities and frustrate attempts at rapprochement."

Yet Havel and his friends persisted in seeking out artistic freedom. In defiance of his official sanctions, Havel and his friends organized a 1975 production of his play, *The Beggar's Opera*. He had written the script in 1972, but it had never been performed. A friend of Havel's, actor and director Andrej Krob, proposed doing the play in secret. Krob would direct and the lead actor, Victor Spousta, scouted out a site for the performance. It was U Celikovskych, a pub and restaurant on the eastern outskirts of Prague. The biggest room in the

For The Beggar's Opera, *John Gay developed a new genre called the ballad opera. This satiric, comical form, using some of the conventions of opera as well as contemporary ballads, has been a popular inspiration for playwrights and composers for centuries. Artist William Hogarth painted this scene from* The Beggar's Opera *in 1728, the year the play was first performed.* (Tate Gallery, London)

restaurant was cleared and sealed off with mattresses to dampen the pub noise and slow the secret police should they storm the event.

The play is an adaptation of an early eighteenth-century musical by British playwright John Gay. In the original tale, a swashbuckling highwayman named Macheath is turned in to the police by a rival, who happens to be his love interest's father. Macheath escapes by seducing another woman, and the two women battle over his affections. In Havel's version, there is no music and no tidy comic ending. The world of the play is one of deception and immorality. To behave morally in this world—not to inform on a friend, not to take advantage of another's misfortune—is pure folly. Macheath is still the lead character, locked in a fierce struggle for control of the criminal underworld with Peachum, his wife's father. Betrayal begets betrayal, until finally in the end the police inspector—who was working for Peachum anyway—takes over the underworld himself and eliminates the other two.

The play—performed under extreme duress because of official sanction—was a disaster technically, but a success dramatically. "The laughter and delight of the audience seemed endless," Havel recalled later. "I told the troupe that I had more joy from this premiere than from all my foreign premieres, from New York to Tokyo." Havel was understandably moved. None of his plays had been performed in Czechoslovakia since 1968, and none would be again until after 1989, and he was finding it increasingly hard to write with no hope of seeing his work on stage. The success of *The Beggar's Opera* was a tremendous lift to his spirits.

The performance was not without consequences, however. When word got out, Havel and his associates were interrogated and the theatrical world was told that because of Havel's defiance "the cultural policy of the government would be much more stringent, and the whole theater community would suffer." As Havel noted, "many a shallow-minded actor fell for it and got very upset at me and my amateur actors for frustrating their artistic ambition, by which, of course, they meant their well-paid sprints from job to job."

Havel was encouraged by the stir he had created. It also got him over his writer's block. He quickly set to work and wrote the one-act play *Audience*. Based on Havel's experience working at the brewery, the play marks the first appearance of Havel's recurring and semi-autobiographical character, Vanek. In *Audience* Vanek, a writer, is working in a brewery, where he is summoned to the office of the foreman. The foreman proceeds to pour out his drunken, paranoid, and self-loathing heart to the reticent Vanek. The foreman's treatment of Vanek alternates between abusive and warm, and betrays an uneasy feeling about the intellectual turned blue-collar, as he tries to get Vanek to inform on his coworkers. This first Vanek play, though not performed in Czechoslovakia, became a huge international success and was performed in theaters all over the world. Havel and his friend, the playwright Pavel Landovsky, made homemade recordings of the play, which were later smuggled out of Czechoslovakia and made into a record by a Swedish company. The tapes then found their way back into the country and became an underground sensation. "For example," Havel recalled, "I once picked up a hitchhiker and, without knowing who I was, he began to quote passages from that play. Or I'd be sitting in a

Havel's play Audience *would not be staged in his home country until 1990, but it was performed worldwide for nearly fifteen years before that. This image is from a production of the play in Poland in 1989.* (Courtesy of Getty Images.)

pub and I'd hear young people shouting lines from the play to each other across the room." Not only did this unanticipated success encourage Havel's return to productive writing, but, as he put it, "it suggested to me that even a playwright who is cut off from his theater can still have an impact on his own domestic milieu."

In April of 1975 Havel, inspired by his dramatic output, decided to make a foray into the political realm. He wrote an open letter to President and First Secretary Gustav Husák, criticizing the government and calling for reforms: "Why are people in fact behaving in the way they do? Why do they do all these things that, taken together, form the impressive image of a totally united society giving total support to its government? . . . they are driven to it by fear." Havel went on to describe the conditions of Late Socialism, the term for life after the Prague Spring, in detail. He admitted that the "most brutal forms of pressure exerted by the authorities on the public are, fortunately, past history" but insisted that "today, oppression takes more subtle and selective forms":

> for fear of losing his job, the schoolteacher teaches things he does not believe; fearing for his future, the pupil repeats them after him . . . fear that . . . his son or daughter will not acquire the necessary total of points for enrollment at a school leads the father to take on all manner of responsibilities and "voluntarily" do everything required. Fear of the consequences of refusal leads people to take part in elections, to vote for the proposed candidates, and to pretend that they regard such ceremonies as genuine elections; out of fear for their livelihood, position or prospects, they go to meetings, vote for every resolution they have to, or at least keep silent: it is fear that carries them through humiliating acts of self-criticism and . . . fear that someone might inform against them prevents them from giving public, and often even private expression to their true opinions.

Havel then addressed Husák directly: "your responsibility as a political leader is still a great one. You help to determine the climate in which we all have to live and can therefore directly influence the final size of the bill our society will be paying for today's process of consolidation." Havel closed by adding, "as a citizen of this country, I hereby request, openly and publicly, that you and the leading representatives of the present regime consider seriously the matters to which I have tried to draw your attention, that you assess in their light the degree of your historic responsibility, and act accordingly."

The letter was printed and passed around by hand, smuggled abroad, and broadcast back into Czechoslovakia on Western radio stations. Later it would be credited as one of the sparks that began the dissident movement that would help to end Communist control. It became a symbol of resistance to Communist totalitarianism. The letter provided Havel, he said, with "a kind of autotherapy," but it also made him famous.

seven

THE SPIRIT
OF '77

Havel's letter to Husák was a precursor to his future
political activities. In 1976 Havel was introduced to
Ivan Jirous, the artistic director of an underground
music group called The Plastic People of the Universe.
The "underground" in an open society is outside of
mainstream culture. In Czechoslovakia, under communism, the underground was more extreme. The Plastic
People of the Universe's music was an explicit violation of
the state prohibitions on importing Western culture. Jirous
and his band could have been arrested and imprisoned.

Before meeting Jirous, Havel had a negative opinion
of the underground because of the stories he had heard
that it was merely self-indulgent. Firsthand experience
changed his views: "there was a disturbing magic in the
music, and a kind of inner warning. Here was something

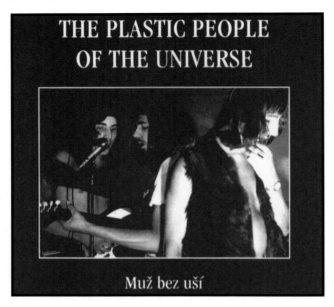

THE PLASTIC PEOPLE OF THE UNIVERSE

Muž bez uší

Heavily influenced by Frank Zappa and The Velvet Underground, The Plastic People of the Universe are often considered one of the most important bands of the twentieth century for their role in the fight for artistic freedom in Communist Czechoslovakia.

serious and genuine, an internally free articulation of an existential experience that everyone who had not become completely obtuse must understand." Soon after meeting Havel, Jirous, his band, and some friends were arrested. Havel felt compelled to help them. "Something ought to be done when someone is unjustly arrested," he said. Even more so because this particular arrest, as Havel described it,

> was not a settling of accounts with political enemies, who to a certain extent were prepared for the risks they were taking. This case had nothing whatsoever to do with a struggle between two competing political cliques. It was something far worse: an attack by the totalitarian system on life itself, on the very essence of

human freedom and integrity. The objects of this
attack were not veterans of old political battles; they
had no political past, or even any well-defined political
positions. They were simply young people who wanted
to live in their own way, to make music they liked . .
. to express themselves in a truthful way.

Havel called an old collaborator from *Tvár*, Jiri Nemec,
for help. While Havel had become something of a public
intellectual, Nemec had taken the underground route.
Havel later claimed their work together trying to free The
Plastic People of the Universe helped to enrich both their
perspectives. They wrote an open letter denouncing the
arrests, and circulated a petition with over seventy
signatures. The signatures were obtained from artists
and writers, but also from lawyers and former party
functionaries. The spectrum of those who opposed the
arrests was surprisingly wide. Czechoslovak society
was beginning to stir again after the crackdown of 1968.
As Havel put it, "this was a time when we were beginning
to learn how to walk upright again, a time of 'exhaustion
with exhaustion,' a time when many different groups of
people had had enough of their isolation and felt that,
if something was going to change, they had to start
looking beyond their own horizons."

The pressure exerted by Havel and Nemec seemed to
work. Of the nineteen people arrested with The Plastic
People of the Universe, only four were actually put in
jail, and these received relatively light sentences. What
really made an impression on Havel was how such a

diverse group of people came together to defend the interests of an obscure group of musicians: "Nemec and I both felt that something had happened here, something that should not be allowed simply to evaporate and disappear but which ought to be transformed into some kind of action that would have a more permanent impact."

A meeting was held on December 10, 1976, attended by Havel, Jiri Nemec, the playwright Pavel Kohout, former Communist Central Committee member Zdenek Mlynár, and historian Vendelin Komeda. At later meetings they were joined by the dissident writer Petr Uhl, former Dubcek foreign minister Jiri Hájek, and journalist Ludvik Vaculik. The group decided not only to form a more permanent organization for protest, but also to broaden their effort and make it a "citizen's initiative." They decided to base their protests on the U.N. Covenants on Civil, Political, Economic, Cultural, and Social Rights, which the Czechoslovak government had signed in Helsinki in 1975.

These agreements were the first international treaties to explicitly mention human rights. Though the U.N. Covenants were not legally binding, Havel's group wanted to exert moral pressure on the Czechoslovak government by pointing out that it should have lived up to the documents it had signed. The group, dubbed "Charter 77" by Pavel Kohout, decided to elect three spokesmen.

Havel and Jiri Hájek were chosen as two of the spokesmen. Havel and Nemec nominated Jan Patocka as the third. Patocka, probably the greatest Czech philosopher of the twentieth century, had dedicated his life to problems of politics, morality, and the human condition. His focus was on living what he called "a life in truth," a concept that would prove extremely influential to Havel. Havel and Nemec felt that Patocka "could impress upon the Charter a moral dimension." Though he was almost seventy years old at the time, and felt personally that there were others more deserving of the position, Patocka agreed, and the Charter had its first group of spokesmen.

The group's next objective was to gather signatures on a manifesto they had put together. As secretly as possible, they collected signatures throughout the holiday season. By early January they had about 1,200 names. "The Charter Declaration" was published on January 7, 1977. It became an international sensation and made headlines in newspapers all over the world, including *Le Monde*, *The London Times*, and the *Frankfurter Allgemeine Zeitung*, which published the text in its entirety. Charter 77 charged the Czech government with abandoning the International Covenant on Civil and Political Rights, and the International Covenant on Economic, Social, and Cultural Rights, which, as the text pointed out, "were signed on behalf of our republic in 1968, reiterated in Helsinki in 1975 and came into force in our country on 23 March 1976."

The Charter 77 declaration pointed out that "basic human rights in our country exist, regrettably, on paper alone," and went on to list the many violations of human rights and freedoms observed by the chartists. The text insisted that The Charter "does not aim . . . to set out its on platform of political or social reform or change, but within its own field of impact to conduct a constructive dialogue with the political and state authorities, particularly by drawing attention to individual cases where human and civil rights are violated, to . . . suggest remedies . . . to reinforce such rights and machinery for protecting them."

Initially, the Czech government suspected that Charter 77 was part of a Western plot hatched from outside the country. They denounced it loudly—inadvertently giving Charter 77 a boost of publicity. The government then tried to enlist the help of figures loyal to the regime to denounce the Charter. They also began a negative campaign to smear the known members of the Charter, particularly Havel. There was even a piece of radio commentary called *Who is Václav Havel?* that described him as an arrogant nobody who held everyone around him in contempt. When these efforts backfired, the authorities turned to the one method they were comfortable with: violence.

The state had no idea how to handle the media sensation caused by the Charter, but they still had a monopoly on power. They rounded up the suspects and began interrogating them. During the interrogations extreme psychological pressure was employed. The

Opposite: *Havel, dressed in his bathrobe, speaks from at his home in Hrádecek on May 26, 1978, in his capacity as spokesperson for the Charter 77 group.* (Courtesy of STF/AFP/Getty Images.)

detainees were questioned at length, made very uncomfortable, berated, and coerced into making compromising or contradictory statements whenever possible. The whole time period was a blur for Havel: "There were interrogations that went on all day long in Ruzyne [a prison near where Havel lived], but initially everyone was released for the night, and we'd all gather . . . to compare notes, draft various texts, meet with foreign correspondents, and make telephone calls . . . so ten hours and sometimes longer of being bombarded with questions by investigators was followed by this hectic activity, which wouldn't let up until late at night."

The dissidents became heroes in the anti-Communist West. The foreign press covered Charter 77 extensively and the foreign attention put intense pressure on the Czech government. In March, Jan Patocka met with the Foreign Minister of the Netherlands, the first official meeting between a Western diplomat and a member of a dissident group. After the meeting Patocka was interrogated so intensely by the secret police he suffered a massive brain hemorrhage soon afterward and died.

Patocka's funeral, which more than a thousand people attended, was a massive show of support for the man who lent moral authority to the Charter 77 movement. At the same time, it was an opportunity for the secret police to frisk, intimidate, and observe the Chartists and their supporters. A police helicopter drowned out the priest, and the service was interrupted several times.

When it became clear that these intimidation tactics

were not working, the authorities charged Havel with crimes against the state. The authorities were trying to silence the Charter 77 group. They hoped that putting Havel behind bars would have that effect.

During Havel's first prison sentence, he continued to write and the Charter continued to function. During his time in prison Havel told his interrogators that he intended to step down as Charter spokesman—not because of any external pressure, but because it had been agreed that spokesmen would serve only for a limited time, so new people could rotate in. It was not a wise move. The authorities published his comment and claimed he had turned on the Charter 77 group. Their goal was to undercut his reputation and silence his voice. When he was freed Havel would have to work to regain his credibility.

When Havel was released, he filed suit against the journalist who had written the defamatory _Who is Václav Havel?_ and set to work undoing the damage inflicted by the negative publicity. He issued statements and helped to found a group called VONS (The Czechoslovak Committee for the Defense of the Unjustly Prosecuted), dedicated to working on specific cases of government persecution. Perhaps his most effective response came in a 1979 essay titled, "The Power of the Powerless." The essay had originally been intended for a proposed symposium between Charter 77 members and Polish intellectuals committed to the defense of human rights. The symposium never happened because in May 1979 Havel

Jan Patocka, reknowned philosopher and cospokesperson for the Charter 77 group until his death in 1977. (Library of Congress)

and ten other members of VONS were arrested. After the arrests the Czech contributors to the symposium rushed their essays into print.

Havel's essay, dedicated to Jan Patocka and directly inspired by his thought, was an attempt to explain the origins and context of the Charter 77 movement. He describes Czechoslovakia as being "post-totalitarian," a country in which individuals, in order to survive, are forced to obey the rules of ideological indoctrination and thereby contribute to the apparent uniformity and pervasiveness of the system. But underneath the ideological façade there existed a layer of real life. The system, Havel wrote, "works only as long as people are willing to live within the lie." The focus of Havel's argument was on what he called "pre-political" actions and events that defy the basic dishonesty of the post-totalitarian state. Because that state was closed to true political debate Havel renounced his 1968 call for the formation of an opposition party. In a state that demanded absolute conformity, he said, acts of everyday defiance, no matter how small, were overtly political. These acts, which could include everything from the fulfillment of basic material needs, to "the simple longing of people to live their own lives in dignity," Havel called "living within the truth," and were made political because they happened in a politically oppressive state.

Havel claimed that groups such as Charter 77, whose origins lay not in politics but in the defense of human dignity were the foundations of a "parallel polis," a separate state within the state where human life could be given a truer expression. He was against the formation of political parties as a means of expression of dissent because he felt that political parties inevitably gave rise to the same ideological falsehoods that existed in the current regime. He also resisted the notion that dissidents were some kind of special class of person. "A dissident" wrote Havel, "is simply a physicist, a sociologist, a worker, a poet, individuals who are doing what they feel they must and, consequently, who find themselves in open conflict with the regime. This conflict has not come about through any conscious intention on their part, but simply through the inner logic of their thinking, behavior, or work."

Havel's essay would later be criticized on intellectual

grounds—he was not a skilled philosopher—but it was successful at galvanizing the movement. Copies of it were printed clandestinely and circulated throughout Eastern Europe. A member of the Polish workers' movement Solidarity—which, led by the charismatic Lech Walesa, would eventually triumph over communism in that country—later reflected, "reading it gave us the theoretical underpinnings for our activity. It maintained our spirits . . . when I look at the victories of Solidarity and Charter 77, I see in them an astonishing fulfillment of the prophecies and knowledge contained in Havel's essay." "The Power of the Powerless" became the intellectual manifesto of resistance movements in all of Eastern Europe.

eight
LIVING IN TRUTH IN PRISON

On May 29, 1979, the secret police arrested Havel. He would be held until January of 1983, his longest stint in prison. He would be severely tested by the experience. His prison routine was strictly monitored. Only family members were allowed to visit, and then only four times per year. Though his brother Ivan would joke that this meant he saw Václav more than usual, it was a very lonely period. Reflecting later, Havel said "by the very nature of things in prison, you're forced to think a little more about yourself, about the meaning of your actions, about questions pertaining to your own Being."

Not only did Havel have to deal with solitude and loneliness, he was frequently unwell with colds, influenza, and painful hemorrhoids. He was a political prisoner, jailed as an enemy of the state. He was made to do hard labor and worked as a welder, in a laundry, and in a scrap metal plant.

Havel was allowed to write letters, though the prison authorities strictly censored the content. Havel's letters were not ordinary missives, and would eventually form a book titled *Letters to Olga*. After his release, Havel said "it's true you won't find many heartfelt, personal passages specifically addressed to my wife in my prison letters. Even so, I think Olga is their main hero, though admittedly she's a hidden hero." "Hidden hero" might be a good way to describe Olga in general, of whom Havel also said "there is one certainty in my life that nothing—so far at least—has been able to shake. That certainty is Olga."

Though Havel was very dependent on his wife, he also used his letters to her to reach out to his girlfriends. During the course of their marriage, Havel had a number of affairs, and Olga knew about most of them. In several letters he asks Olga to send a kiss to Andulka, Havel's nickname for Anna Kohoutova, the mistress whose bed he was dragged from the morning of his arrest, and in another he describes a dream in which he is seduced by an ex-lover.

Olga was determined to keep their marriage together. But Havel's relationship with Jitka Vodnanská, a beautiful social psychologist whom he met just before going to prison, seriously tested Olga's commitment.

Havel and Vodnanská were lovers for six years following his long stint in prison. Olga responded by taking up with a young actor, Jan Kaspar. Olga and Kaspar were very much in love, and thought eventually she decided to leave Kaspar and return to Havel, her affair was a tremendous blow to her husband. Havel seems to have relied on Olga to be utterly constant and the news of her affair knocked a support that he had grown dependent upon out from under him.

Havel's prison term was interrupted by a serious medical crisis in January 1983. He collapsed with a wildly beating heart and extremely high fever. He sent

Havel (second from left) is visited in the hospital by his wife Olga (far right), his brother Ivan (second from right), and other members of the Charter 77 movement, Jiri (far left) and Jan Ruml, February 1983. (AP Photo/CTK)

a desperate message to Olga, who rushed to the prison with a friend. When they were refused visitation they sent word of his illness to friends abroad, who helped get the news out. The foreign press wrote stories about Havel's illness and the government began to fear the repercussions of Havel dying in prison. There had been growing signs that Havel would soon be released in any case. His imprisonment had done nothing to diminish his role as a dissident. As Havel said, "they realized I was a bigger political liability as a prisoner than I would be as a free man."

Havel was transferred to a hospital and told that his sentence was being terminated. His immediate reaction was panic. He actually asked if he could spend one more night in prison. He had simply become so accustomed to confinement that the idea of freedom was frightening. However, once he arrived in the civilian hospital he was in a state of euphoria: "That month in the hospital was probably the most beautiful month of my life. Released from the burden of prison, but not yet encumbered by the burden of freedom, I lived like a king." Havel was told he could do whatever he wanted in the hospital if only he would agree not to talk to the foreign press. Visiting hours, therefore, did not apply to him, and he was allowed to stay up until all hours carousing with the nurses, who doted on the dissident playwright: "just imagine—you scarcely see a woman for four years, and suddenly they plop you down among ten fresh nursing-school grads!"

Havel was allowed to stay in the hospital longer than was medically necessary because the government was embarrassed by the timing of his release. Voice of America Radio had broadcast an appeal for his release only the day before it happened and the regime did not want to appear to have buckled to international pressure. But as Havel realized, "the beautiful dream had to end. The day came when I had to step back into the world as it really was."

That day came in March of 1983, and it was followed by a severe case of post-prison depression. Havel began his affair with Vodnanská, became morose, drank heavily, slept badly, and began to withdraw from the world. His dark mood is reflected in the work he produced during that time period. *Largo Desolato* was published in 1984. Like many of Havel's plays, it was produced in *samizdat* form, which meant that only a few copies of the book were printed and then handed out to trusted individuals, who in turn made copies and passed them on. *Samizdat* was the only way to publish for authors who had been blacklisted, or who wanted to get their work abroad for publication in exile or Western journals.

Largo Desolato is the story of Dr. Leopold Kopriva, an existential philosopher whose work had landed him on the state's enemies list. He is constantly harassed by the secret police and pressured by fairweather friends and supporters who want him to do more to speak out against the regime. He begins to develop a pathological fear of his own capitulation. His works have violated section 511 of the penal code, and he is being pressured to confess his guilt. He talks constantly of human identity and how to maintain it in the face of powers that would obliterate it, but his own identity has already been eroded completely. He drinks constantly, eats only to stay alive, and paces the floor of his apartment, looking for excuses not to write. Two workers who bring by stolen sheaves of writing paper can't get him over his writer's block. When an attractive young student confesses her love for him over a glass of rum, he is incapable of responding. The play ends with Kopriva pushed to the brink of desperation by the secret police, who tell him that his case has been "adjourned indefinitely for the time being," leaving him in the perpetual state of desperate uncertainty that has reduced him to near-nothingness.

Havel's post-prison experience would reach a turning point with his next play, *Temptation*. The writing process was difficult at first and Havel threw out whole scenes he had written, but he took only ten days to finish the play once the words started flowing. Where *Largo Desolato* was a meditation on the erosion of human identity under despotic oppression, *Temptation* was about the dangers of flirting with the power that does the oppressing.

Havel had often been tempted by the authorities. He had been offered his own journal in return for cooperation during the *Tvár* affair, and he was given many opportunities in prison to capitulate in exchange for renouncing his dissident stance. He was often wracked by guilt that his political activities were harming those

Many versions of the Faust story exist, all concerning a negotiated pact between man and the devil, involving human hubris and diabolic cunning. The cautionary tale has been frequently dramatized. This vivid poster from 1889 promotes a theatrical rendition of Goethe's version, performed in New York City. (Library of Congress)

close to him, or that he had placed all those who signed Charter 77 in jeopardy.

Temptation is based on the medieval legend of the man who sells his soul to the devil. This tale is embodied

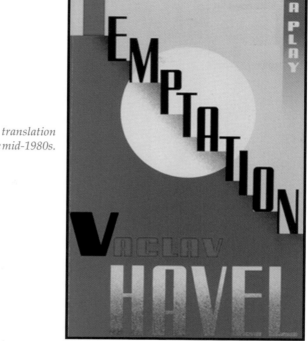

An English-language translation of Havel's play from the mid-1980s.

in the story of Dr. Faustus, which has been told in various operas, novels, and poems, by authors such as Christopher Marlowe, Johann Wolfgang von Goethe, and Thomas Mann.

For his play Havel created a contemporary character called Dr. Henry Foustka, a respected scientist working at a research institute. As with the organizations in most Havel plays, the institute is a dull series of meaningless procedures, structures, and rituals. The staff, whose task it is to produce, deploy, and protect the scientific truth, hardly notice one another and are numbed by routine. Their days are filled with idle chit-chat and calls for more coffee. The Director's most interesting query to his staff is "Did you sleep well?" or "Do you have any problems?" He shows no genuine interest in the answer.

The action of the play takes place against the backdrop of a pending social event the institute is throwing for its employees. The event is not just a party, but a scientific way of combating "the various interpersonal problems that crop up among us from time to time." Meanwhile, Dr. Foustka—a paragon of scientific knowledge—is in his apartment in the midst of an arcane ritual involving an ancient tome, candles, and a circle drawn in chalk. He is interrupted by a bizarre visitor called Fistula who seems to know everything about him. Fistula warns Foustka that he is aware of all the details of Foustka's secret dabbling in the occult but suggests he could be of assistance to the scientist: "You . . . have only three options: you can continue to consider me an *agent provocateur* and insist that I leave. Secondly, not to think of me in those terms but instead to trust me. Thirdly, not to make your mind up in this matter just yet and adopt a waiting posture . . . if I may, I'd recommend the third alternative."

Foustka is perturbed by his guest, then outraged, then finally compliant. He is still not sure he can trust Fistula, but the third alternative is the only one that requires him not to take a stand or give anything up. In the end, Fistula gets him to agree to a pact whereby Fistula will help Foustka, and Foustka will agree to cover for Fistula should they be found out. Fistula is very obviously playing the role of the devil, and Foustka is succumbing to his temptations.

The next day at work, the Director confronts the staff with the revelation that one of their number has been engaged in ritualistic and pre-scientific activities. He points the finger at Foustka in front of everyone. Foustka begs forgiveness, saying he was only dabbling in the occult to better understand and combat it. He is given another chance, but Fistula comes calling again, angry that Foustka has broken their agreement by capitulating to the institute. Foustka embarks on a dizzying series of lies and deceptions only to discover that Fistula has been the Director's agent all along.

Temptation ends vaguely. The audience is led to believe that Foustka is destroyed, but it is not clear whether he is imprisoned, fired, or disgraced. It is typical of Havel's writing that the audience is left with serious ambiguities. *Temptation's* allegorical underpinnings however, are clear: people cannot compromise themselves to get what they want if they hope to escape with their scruples intact. This was an invaluable lesson to remember when standing up to the Czech state, which sought to implicate everyone in order to maximize compliance and monopolize power. The only way to respond to this system with integrity was to stick to one's principles.

nine

THE VELVET REVOLUTION

During the 1980s the same inflexibility and stagnation that had plagued the Communist countries of Europe in the late 1960s and early 1970s returned. Discontent reached a fever pitch. The United States and the democratic countries of Western Europe were outspending, out-developing, and out-performing the USSR and its satellite lands in almost every area. As the Soviets struggled to keep pace in the arms race, their economy slumped into a second-world status. The Communist ideology was revealed to be inadequate. The same slogans were still used, but no one took them seriously.

In 1985 Mikhail Gorbachev became General Secretary of the Communist Party in the USSR. Gorbachev realized that the economic stagnation of the Communist

Communist-controlled Czechoslovakia in 1985. (University of Texas, Austin)

system could not be changed without political reform. Though he faced opposition from Communist hard-liners who wanted to retrench their position, Gorbachev pushed through his programs of *Glastnost* (openness) and *Perestroika* (reform). He knew he had to move fast before the hard-liners could organize resistance. Later he admitted he had underestimated the effects his reforms would have after seventy years of Communist rule. Gorbachev would eventually preside over the dissolution of the USSR and the collapse of the Communist system in Europe.

The change was not limited to the Soviet Union. In 1980 a dissident worker's movement called Solidarnosc, or "Solidarity," arose in Poland, partially inspired by Havel and Charter 77. The movement was led by a shipyard worker, Lech Walesa, and soon had ten million

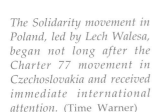

The Solidarity movement in Poland, led by Lech Walesa, began not long after the Charter 77 movement in Czechoslovakia and received immediate international attention. (Time Warner)

members. Walesa would be jailed and released by the Polish government as it tried to deal with demands for reform. By 1989, Solidarnosc would win the right to be a legal organization, and Lech Walesa would eventually become the first freely elected president of Poland.

In Hungary János Kádár, the leader installed by the Soviets after they crushed the rebellion of 1956, began to institute reforms. The Communists did not give up power, but the Hungarian leadership eased restrictions, notably on travel and trade with the West.

The Czechoslovak Communist Party was in sorry shape. Still presided over by Gustav Husák, the hard-line replacement for Alexander Dubcek, the party had been discredited in almost every way. Economically, Czechoslovakia was failing. Industry was stagnant. People were mired in jobs and lacked opportunities. Politically, the party clung to Communist dogma while the world moved rapidly in other directions. Socially, Czechoslovaks had withdrawn into themselves. Self-expression of any kind could incur official sanctions, which created fear and mistrust. The only real legitimacy the government held was control of the military, the secret police, and their web of informers. The secret police monitored people's movements, especially those suspected of anti-government behavior. They made extensive use of informants, ordinary citizens who would inform on their friends, neighbors, and colleagues. This gave the impression that one was being watched at all times, which further demoralized society and caused resentment. In February of 1989 Václav Havel was convicted of the crime of "standing in the street" during a political protest. After serving several months of his nine-month sentence, he was released under heavy public pressure in May.

The government's ability to control the populace had begun to erode, though officially there was no softening of the party's position. The situation was heading toward a crisis. On Friday, November 17, 1989, a crowd of 15,000 students gathered outside the Pathology Institute in Prague to commemorate the death of Jan Opletal, a student killed by the Nazis fifty years earlier. The students had official permission to gather—Opletal was a state-approved martyr—but there was more afoot than a state-sanctioned vigil. The group was not allowed to march from the Pathology Institute to Wenceslas Square in central Prague. When the students decided to head for the square anyway they were met by riot police, who waded into the crowd swinging truncheons. The crowd marched defiantly on, increasing in size as it went. By the time they reached the National Theater, en route to Wenceslas Square, the number of demonstrators had swelled to 50,000. Actors and waiters, café patrons and local residents joined the ranks.

A young dissident named John Bok was dragged from the crowd and arrested. Bok was an acquaintance of Havel's (he would become his unofficial security chief in the coming weeks). As he was dragged away by riot police, Bok shouted to friends to call Havel, who was at his cottage at Hrádecek. Havel rushed back to Prague, arriving around midnight to reports of police brutality and spontaneous acts of rebellion. Statues were defaced, vigils and meetings were held all over town at pubs, theaters, flats, and cafés. The government issued a statement downplaying the number of casualties and arrests and said that order had been restored and the protestors treated with restraint. Meanwhile, the Western media broadcast said that a bloody insurrection had broken out in Prague, that Prague Castle was surrounded by tanks,

Havel works in his office in Prague in October, 1989, just weeks before becoming president of Czechoslovakia. (Courtesy of PASCAL GEORGE/AFP/Getty Images.)

and that a young student had been killed in the melee. This latter piece of news, though it later proved to be erroneous, galvanized the protesters and intensified their resistance to the authorities. As word of a "massacre" spread, so did the uprising. The Velvet Revolution had begun.

Once he arrived back in Prague, Havel flung himself into the movement. He sped from meetings, marches, and rallies, working to organize the revolutionary elements into a coalition. On Sunday, November 19, 1989, at 11 PM, a gathering of Charter 77 veterans, VONS participants, banned church groups, and members of various Czechoslovak resistance organizations met. They voted unanimously to form an umbrella organization called Civic Forum.

Aimed at avoiding a repeat of the repression of 1968, Civic Forum issued a proclamation calling for an independent investigation into the 'massacre,' the punishment of those responsible, the resignation of several key government officials, and the release of all political prisoners. Havel placed himself at the center of the movement. He worked tirelessly from morning until far into the night, coordinating committees of Civic Forum, building coalitions, holding meetings, and keeping close tabs on events. He set up headquarters for Civic Forum in the Magic Lantern Theater in Prague. There he gathered a team of experts and began planning the future of the country. Havel gave regular press conferences to an eager and excited foreign press corps, speaking of Civic Forum's desire to replace the corrupt and totalitarian Socialist state with a pluralist democracy. He began to take on the role and the responsibilities of the leader of the opposition.

When Milos Jakes, the First Secretary of the Czechoslovak Communist Party, announced his resignation along with the resignation of his Politburo (central committee) and Secretariat, on November 24, 1989, Havel and his supporters took this news as a sign that the party was imploding. There had been fear that there would be a government crackdown. An ominous precedent had recently been set in China, where the Communist regime answered peaceful demonstrators in

Tiananmen Square with tanks, tear gas, and bullets. The debacle was shown live on international television, and made an enormous impact on the international scene.

This was not to be the case in Czechoslovakia. The name Velvet Revolution evokes the surprisingly peaceful nature of the events there. It also represents the spirit behind the revolution. The name comes from the 1960s rock group, The Velvet Underground, an experimental band led by Lou Reed. The band was a favorite of Havel's and a major influence on underground musicians in Czechoslovakia during the Communist era. The Velvet Revolution was almost entirely peaceful—one of the most surprisingly bloodless revolutions in history— and was led by a group of long-haired, suede-jacket-wearing intellectuals whose inspiration came more from the Sixties counterculture than from traditional politics. There was a very real possibility that violence would break out at any moment. However, Havel and his supporters reasoned that without Soviet support—which had been behind the crackdown in 1968—the Communists could not muster the strength or will to repress the popular uprising. After all, the Soviets had not intervened when Communist regimes collapsed in Hungary and Poland. This figured heavily in the calculations of Havel and Civic Forum, who chose to challenge the regime.

One of Havel's first political masterstrokes came during a huge rally on November 26, the day after Jakes's resignation. Following Alexander Dubcek to the microphone, dressed in his best Bohemian café artist

Dubcek and Havel join hands, accompanied by dissident pop singer Marta Kubisova, as they walk to address a rally of two hundred thousand protesters gathered in Prague's Wenceslas Square, on November 24, 1989. (Courtesy of LUBOMIR KOTEK/AFP/Getty Images.)

outfit, Havel told the gathering that Civic Forum would build a bridge from totalitarianism to democracy. He called for "truth, humanity, freedom as well." Havel emphasized that the nation was now truly in the hands of its citizens, over a million of whom applauded wildly with every statement he made. Havel then turned the stage over to Ladislav Adamec, the Communist prime minister of Czechoslovakia.

Adamec was a moderate who had brokered a deal with Civic Forum to speak at the demonstration in hopes of easing tensions. He was initially greeted with cheers from the hopeful crowd, which saw in his presence a sign that the regime might cooperate. But Adamec, in true Communist fashion, refused to recant the central role of the Communist Party, and the crowd responded by drowning him out with whistles and boos. Adamec had hoped that by speaking to the crowd he could salvage the role of the Communist Party in a reformed state. Instead, he had to be pulled from the podium to avoid an anti-government riot.

The fate of the Communist Party was sealed. On November 29 the government was forced to remove Article 4 of the Czechoslovak constitution, which guaranteed the leading role of the Communist Party. This effectively ended the Communist domination of the government that had begun in 1948. Barely ten days after it had begun spontaneously in the streets of Prague, the Velvet Revolution had brought an end to Communist rule in Czechoslovakia.

Havel stepped quickly and decisively into the void created by the disintegration of Communist rule. In early December, Civic Forum members debated about whom they should put forth as a candidate for the presidency. Some wanted Dubcek, while others thought Havel was the natural choice. There were several possibilities discussed, but Havel seized the opportunity to put himself forward—coyly stating that, while he did not want the presidency, he would undertake the job for the sake of the nation.

Opposite: Standing on a balcony of Prague Castle, Havel flashes a victory sign to a crowd of thousands after being elected president of Czechoslovakia on December 29, 1989. (AP Photo/Diether Endlicher)

On December 10, Civic Forum announced his official nomination as their candidate, but Havel still had to convince the National Assembly—whose Communist members were hostile towards him—that he was a viable candidate. The National Assembly, which was still controlled by Communists, wanted to have a direct popular vote to elect the president. Civic Forum feared this would cripple Havel, who did not have the same name recognition as the Communist candidates who had controlled the media for forty years. Havel argued for an election by the Assembly and set about raising his profile though a deal he negotiated with the director of Czechoslovak Television. Havel demanded the station director give him airtime to promote himself. He read a statement live during the evening news on December 16.

His next obstacle to overcome was Alexander Dubcek. Dubcek, though he had been relegated to obscurity for years, was still a household name in Czechoslovakia. He was associated with the Prague Spring of 1968 and, as a Slovak, would guarantee strong support from Slovakia for the new government. Havel went to Dubcek and made a proposal. If Dubcek would support Havel's bid for the presidency, Havel would support Dubcek's appointment as head of the Federal Assembly and his candidacy for president in the next free elections. They also agreed to keep their pact a secret. Dubcek was appointed head of the Assembly on December 28, and the next day he introduced fifty-three-year-old Václav Havel as president of the Czechoslovak Federal Republic.

Dubcek upheld his end of the bargain. In the years to come, he would stand by Havel's side and make many public statements supporting the new president. Havel never returned the favor. Though he supported Dubcek's appointment to the Assembly, his only gesture toward supporting Dubcek for president was a vague assertion that at some point a Slovak ought to occupy the position. This was never to be, and Dubcek would die as the result of a car accident in 1992 without ever contesting Havel's presidency.

ten

THE VELVET DIVORCE

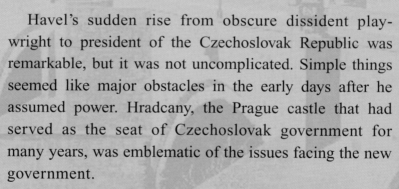

Havel's sudden rise from obscure dissident playwright to president of the Czechoslovak Republic was remarkable, but it was not uncomplicated. Simple things seemed like major obstacles in the early days after he assumed power. Hradcany, the Prague castle that had served as the seat of Czechoslovak government for many years, was emblematic of the issues facing the new government.

The castle was a symbol of authoritarian rule. It sits high above the city, magisterially overlooking the subjects who live below. It seemed bizarre that the new democratic leader of the country should preside, as kings and dictators had done, from such a perch. It was enormous, dark, and out of date in almost every way. Havel must have felt very out of place there at first. He

Prague's magestic castle, Hradcany, built on a steep hill overlooking the Vltava River in the ninth century, had been the seat of non-democratic rulers for centuries, including the eras of the Holy Roman Empire and the Austro-Hungarian Empire. (Liber chronicarum CCXXX, 1493)

was a dissident, a fan of rock and roll, and his blue jeans and suede jackets were not the formal attire of a states-man. He had to borrow a suit for his first public appear-ances as president. But Havel would get used to the trappings of power.

He hired theater professionals to redesign the castle. Havel's office was overhauled, the castle guards were given new uniforms, Tomás Masaryk's library was re-stored, and paintings by contemporary artists replaced the works of socialist realism that had adorned the walls. There was still the matter of the imperious nature of the building, but Havel did not flinch from this; in fact, he embraced it. Instead of seeking out overtly democratic gestures—reaffirming the parliamentary nature of the government or the rule of law—Havel seemed to fancy the idea of a "crowned republic." He organized a New Year's performance of *Te Deum*, a piece by Czech composer Antonin Dvorák, in St. Vitus's Cathedral in Prague, at which he would make his formal presentation as the new head of state. It seemed very much like a coronation. Havel commissioned an official biography by his friend, the writer Edá Kriseová. The book was roundly criticized for lauding Havel to the extent that the facts were lost or distorted.

Havel was convinced that the consolidation of power in the newborn republic required an outward show of majesty, a flourish that would galvanize the people behind their new leader. While Havel draped himself in the trappings of power, he did not resemble a typical head of state. He was still more Bohemian artist than dignified statesman. He wore his hair long, and cultivated the radical image of the sixties and seventies. As president, he received foreign celebrities at the castle, but these were not typical dignitaries. Havel's early guests included Lou Reed, founder of The Velvet Underground, The Rolling Stones, actress and activist Jane Fonda, musician Frank Zappa, and British playwright Harold Pinter. His guest list represented some of the most popular, daring, and progressive artists of the past two decades.

The effect of liberation from communism on the entire country mirrored the changes at Hradcany. The nation began to wake up from its slumber. With freedom of expression restored, people could read, write, play, or watch whatever they wanted. The command economy of the Communists was gone and people were free to start their own businesses. Václav Klaus, a free market economist and member of Civic Forum, would emerge as the leader of a radical privatization movement, which sought to put all the collective industry and property in private hands as quickly as possible. The times were marked by a pressing drive to change things as rapidly as possible, and also by a sense of disorientation, tumult, and excess brought on by the wholesale reorientation of society.

Havel's early days as president bordered on excess as well, as he and his entourage tried to transform the castle and the country. He rode around in a brand new fleet of BMWs and filled many posts at the castle with his friends and compatriots. He formed a tight circle of advisers who worked up to eighteen hours a day, in order to keep up with the demands of the new government. The Office of Amnesties and Complaints received up to 7,000 letters a month, forcing the administration to hold large public meetings to hear grievances.

All the activity took a toll on Havel. He seemed to grow alienated from the outside world. Friends complained that he was inaccessible and, perhaps more significantly, his colleagues at Civic Forum were isolated from the new president. Civic Forum was working at a fever pitch as well, trying to lay the groundwork for democratic elections. They set up election centers throughout the country, advising people on democratic and parliamentary procedures and encouraging the formation of political groups. Civic Forum eschewed any political affiliation. They insisted that their task was simply to mobilize the populace for the coming challenge of democracy.

Almost as soon as he became president, Havel cut off all ties to Civic Forum. His former dissident associates did not denounce him at first—they sensed that the new republic was too fragile for infighting—but they resented Havel's withdrawal from the group. Many saw it as an attempt to carve out a greater sphere of power for the president, at the expense of the other branches of Czechoslovak government. Havel's penchant for cutting direct deals outside of the democratic process also caused resentment. "These tactics work perfectly well in small groups within a small opposition," said one collaborator, "but it would never have worked within a large opposition like that of Solidarnosc in Poland. And it most certainly never worked during the first months of his presidency, when power was seen simply as manipulation."

Havel's problems came to head in 1990 when he decided, against the advice of his advisers, to address the Parliament regarding the changing of the name of the country. The name was a point of contention for two main reasons. First, it still contained the word 'socialist,' and second, it placed the Czechs ahead of the Slovaks in the title. Slovakia had long resented what it saw as

Czech arrogance and dominance. Havel wanted to change the name to "The Czechoslovak Republic," dropping "socialist" from the title and thus reverting back to the name used before World War II. One problem with this, as an adviser pointed out, was that Havel should not expect the assembly to automatically approve his recommendation. But that is exactly what he tried to do.

The Federal Assembly rejected Havel's proposal. They said it failed to take the nationalist concerns into account, and only served to intensify the Czech-Slovak divide. Havel's gaffe over the name change was only a small piece of the fractious Czech-Slovak issue. The tension between the two republics of the Czechoslovak Federation grew steadily more prevalent.

In spite of the tumult, free elections were organized and held successfully in June of 1990, giving majorities to Civic Forum and its Slovak counterpart, Public Against Violence. The groups, which had been formed as civic organizations, had quickly turned into the chief political parties. Soon, however, these proto-parties broke up into factions. Civic Forum was split between a right-wing group of free-marketers, led by Václav Klaus, and a more left-leaning group that was closer politically to Havel. In 1992, Havel again ran for president, but Slovaks in the Federal Assembly voted to block his election.

Václav Klaus's group won control of the assembly. Klaus began negotiations with Vladimir Meciar, the head of Public Against Violence, on a solution to the Czech-Slovak issue. Klaus thought Slovakia hindered

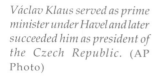

Václav Klaus served as prime minister under Havel and later succeeded him as president of the Czech Republic. (AP Photo)

Czech economic development. He wanted to privatize the country rapidly, and implement free-market reforms. This required a more developed economic structure than Slovakia possessed. He wanted to separate the republic into two countries. Meciar was an ambitious politician, and probably used the Czech-Slovak divide more for political gain than for any ideological reason.

Klaus and Meciar negotiated an end to the Czechoslovak Federal Republic. It was dissolved at midnight on December 31, 1992. Many were elated by the news of the peaceful separation. At the time, a bloody conflict raged in Yugoslavia, a nation that was a synthesis of many ethnic groups formed, much like the Czechoslovak Republic, by international agreement more than natural affinity. Serbs, Croatians, and Bosnian Muslims were exterminating one another, bringing the term "ethnic cleansing" into the world's vocabulary for the first time, and horrifying observers who thought that such atrocities could never occur in Europe again.

Compared to the Yugoslavian situation, the Czecho-Slovak divorce was a model of civility. The news was a crushing blow to Havel, however, who had invested a great deal of energy defending the union and working for its maintenance. It meant the first phase of his political career ended in a resounding failure. He resigned from public life, though he would soon reemerge to become president of the new Czech Republic.

Havel had been immensely popular in the wake of the Velvet Revolution. The Velvet Divorce, the name coined to describe the dissolution of Czechoslovakia, showed that even an icon like Havel could be subject to the ups and downs of politics. However, while it was clear that his status was eroding at home, Havel continued to enjoy enormous popularity abroad. The position of president gave Havel only limited power over domestic affairs, which were overseen by the prime minister. The president had almost total control over foreign affairs, however, and Havel used this to become a major force in world politics. He began a campaign to reintegrate Czechoslovakia, then later the Czech Republic, into Europe.

Havel signed a treaty with Germany to repair some

of the damage done by the expulsions of Germans from Czechoslovakia after World War II. The treaty made reference to the 2.5 million Germans *expelled* from the Sudetenland, a vague but important acknowledgement of Czechoslovak responsibility, which was unpopular with the Czech people, but crucial to establishing ties with economically powerful Germany. The treaty established inter-governmental, economic, scientific, and cultural cooperation between the two nations. The Germans agreed to support Czech membership in the European Community, which would soon become the European Union, and to provide material and logistic support for Czech economic privatization. Havel was a believer in European integration, and he became one of the chief spokesmen for the idea of a European Union. He campaigned for Czech membership in NATO, and made speeches on the subject of European integration in foreign capitals. During his visits he was showered with honors, given honorary degrees by foreign universities, and gained a reputation as the moral voice of Europe.

Havel was a master performer and his performance gained the Czechs standing abroad. Membership in NATO meant that the Czech Republic, once at the heart of Communist Europe, was now a partner of the Western powers they had been allied against in the Warsaw Pact. It meant the Czechs had come back to their founding president Tomás Masaryk's goal of European integration and cosmopolitan collaboration with other nations.

After thirty-two years of marriage, Olga died at the Havel home in Prague on January 27, 1996 at the age of sixty-three. (AP Photo)

Having weathered the tumultuous period following the Velvet Revolution and the Velvet Divorce, Havel was upset by a series of personal crises. In 1996 his wife Olga died of cancer. She had not only been a bastion of support for Havel during his dissident years, she had been a major force in the revitalization of Czechoslovak civil society after the Revolution. Olga did not merely play the role of first lady, attending ceremonies and making public appearances. She involved herself with charitable work. Her foundation, created with the generous financial support of a Czech industrialist, the Good Will Committee, focused on reforming the nation's many Communist-era detention facilities. The foundation grew at a phenomenal rate as donations poured in from abroad and domestically, and was later renamed the Olga Havlová Foundation. Her passing was mourned by the Czechoslovak people as a great loss to the nation.

In November of that year it seemed like Olga's death might precede Václav's by only a short time. Doctors found a spot on the chain-smoking president's lungs. Before the operation to remove it, Havel was seen on television smoking a cigarette with his chief surgeon. Complications resulted from the surgery, and the team of doctors attending to Havel called in an American specialist to save him from recurring pneumonia.

Havel recovered from the illness, but then created a controversy when he married his new girlfriend, an actress named Dagmar Veskrnova, only eight days after being released from the hospital. Not only did the public disapprove of Havel's hasty marriage, which came less than a year after Olga's death, but Dagmar also would prove to be much more controversial than Olga. She enjoyed playing the public role of First Lady, and caused

a major controversy when she called for a legal defini-
tion of her position. She drew the constant ire of the
Czech press, making the president and his wife something of a tabloid sensation. Havel would have continued
health problems in 1997 and 1998, suffering from a
punctured intestine and various other ailments. Nev-
ertheless, he managed to outmaneuver Václav Klaus—
who had become the prime minister—for re-election
as president in 1997. Now in his sixties, he pushed

*Havel waves to onlookers as he enters his villa with actress Dagmar Veskrnova
following their private wedding ceremony in Prague on January 4,1997.* (AP
Photo/Stanislav Peska/CTK)

support of Czech entrance into NATO through the Assembly, a major political victory.

Havel's last term as president was less dramatic. While he continued to enjoy an excellent reputation abroad, he was criticized at home for holding on to power too long. Havel's story is unique in the Eastern European dissident movements. Lech Walesa, the Polish leader of Solidarnosc, would be voted out of office in 1995 in favor of a former Communist. Havel, on the other hand, would serve out his second full term as president, ending his remarkable tenure in 2002. His chief rival, Václav Klaus, would succeed him.

Today, Havel continues to be engaged informally with world politics. He speaks publicly, and has written essays, editorial articles, and other pieces about world events.

Václav Havel's career as a playwright, dissident, and politician has been an epic drama. While his political tenure was not a total triumph, he presided over the most successful transition out of communism of all the former Warsaw Pact nations. More than any other figure, he helped to define the Eastern European resistance against Communist domination. As a rare mix of artist, intellectual, revolutionary, and politician, he is an inspiration to those seeking a model for peaceful political change. Through it all he continued to write. His dramatic work

Opposite: *Photographed here in 2000 at a meeting of the European Parliament in Strasbourg, France, Havel remains active in Czech politics, including the country's bid to become a member of the European Union, which it did in 2004.* (AP Photo)

continues to stand as a substantial accomplishment. Havel may have retired from the political stage, but his performance will not soon be forgotten.

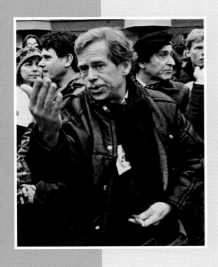

timeline

1936	Václav Havel born on October 5.
1938	Munich Conference between Germany, Italy, England, France annexed the Sudetenland of Czechoslovakia to Hitler in September; Ivan Havel born in October.
1945	Czechoslovakia liberated by Soviet troops.
1948	Communists seize power in Czechoslovakia.
1951	Havel made apprentice to chemist Otto Wichterle; begins meeting with the Thirty-Sixers.
1953	Joseph Stalin dies.
1956	Havel makes his first public appearance at the Young Writer's Conference at Dobris, Czechoslovakia.
1957	Meets Olga Splichalová; begins compulsory service in the Czechoslovak army.
1959	Hired by Jan Werich as a stagehand at the ABC Theater in Prague.
1960	Hired at the Theater on the Balustrade.
1963	First performance of *The Garden Party,* at the Balustrade.
1964	Havel and Olga Splichalová married at town hall in Zizkov district of Prague.
1965	Havel writes the absurdist satire *The Memorandum.*

1968	Alexander Dubcek government begins reforms in Czechoslovakia in May, start of the "Prague Spring" movement of liberalization and reform; Warsaw Pact invasion of Czechoslovakia in August.
1971	Havel becomes a banned author.
1974	Takes a job as a laborer at the Trutnov Brewery.
1975	Writes an open letter to First Secretary of the Czechoslovak Communist Party Gustav Husák.
1976	Charter 77 is formed.
1977	Charter 77 Declaration published in January; Havel arrested for the first time, serves four months in prison.
1979	Publishes "The Power of the Powerless"; arrested again, and this time he serves four years.
1983	Havel released from prison.
1989	Beginning of the Velvet Revolution; Havel introduced as president of the Czechoslovak Republic.
1992	Czechoslovakia dissolved into two separate nations; Havel resigns as Czechoslovakian president, becomes president of the new Czech Republic.
1996	Olga Havlová dies.
1997	Havel wins reelection as president.
2002	Havel's last term in office ends.

sources

CHAPTER ONE: A Twentieth-Century Childhood

p. 20, "On the 9th of May . . ." John Keane, *Václav Havel: A Political Tragedy in Six Acts* (New York: Basic Books, 2000), 63.

CHAPTER TWO: An Education in Communist Czechoslovakia

p. 31, "Václav simply couldn't . . ." Keane, *Václav Havel,* 88.

p. 31, "I longed for . . ." Václav Havel, *Disturbing the Peace: A Conversation with Karel Hvizdála* (New York: Alfred A. Knopf, 1990), 5.

p. 31, "Our family employed . . ." Ibid.

p. 31-32, "I believe this . . ." Ibid., 5-6.

p. 32-33, "I benefited from . . ." Ibid., 6-7.

p. 33, "I have fond . . ." Ibid., 7.

p. 34, "gather around himself . . ." Keane, *Václav Havel,* 103.

p. 34, "came, puffed on . . ." Ibid., 107.

p. 35-36, "When I think . . ." Havel, *Disturbing the Peace,* 24.

p. 36, "You were always . . ." Keane, *Václav Havel,* 93.

p. 40, "the courses did . . ." Havel, *Disturbing the Peace,* 29.

p. 40-42, "My friends and I . . ." Ibid., 26.

p. 42, "These sessions in Kolár's . . ." Ibid., 27.

p. 43, "I wrote a letter . . ." Ibid., 30.

p. 43, "spoiled and pampered . . ." Keane, *Václav Havel,* 128.

p. 43-44, "this confusion reflected . . ." Havel, *Disturbing the Peace,* 32.

p. 44, "my entry into . . ." Ibid., 32-33.

CHAPTER THREE: A Playwright is Born

p. 46-47, "I served with . . ." Havel, *Disturbing the Peace,* 37.

p. 47, "in a way that . . ." Ibid., 38.

p. 49-50, "when the time . . ." Ibid., 38-39.

p. 51, "I wasn't really . . ." Ibid., 39.

p. 51-52, "The season I worked . . ." Ibid., 39-40.

p. 52, "no matter how . . ." Ibid., 44.

p. 54, "but, it didn't . . ." Ibid., 45-46.

p. 54, "The point is that . . ." Václav Havel, *The Garden Party,* in *The Garden Party and Other Plays* (New York: Grove Press, 1993), 19.

p. 55, "Me! You mean . . ." Ibid., 50.

CHAPTER FOUR: Ptydepe

p. 61, "failed again in . . ." Alexander Dubcek, *Hope Dies Last: The Autobiography of Alexander Dubcek,* Jiri Hochman, ed., trans. (New York: Kodansha International, 1993), 112.

p. 62-63, "to tell you . . ." Havel, *Disturbing the Peace,* 75.

p. 63, "their aims appealed . . ." Ibid., 76.

p. 63, "an island of . . ." Ibid., 79.

p. 66, "don't get mixed . . ." Ibid., 83.

p. 66, "someone who lived . . ." Ibid., 77.

p. 66, "it was . . . the . . ." Ibid.

p. 66, "You mind your . . ." Keane, *Václav Havel,* 175.

p. 68-69, "GROSS: What can . . ." Václav Havel, *The Memorandum,* in *The Garden Party and Other Plays* (New York: Grove Press, 1993), 93-94.

p. 70, "attempting to salvage . . ." Ibid., 129.

CHAPTER FIVE: Prague Spring

p. 73, "spring of our . . ." Keane, *Václav Havel,* 194.

p. 73, "I understand 1968 . . ." Havel, *Disturbing the Peace,* 93-94.

p. 75, "Just think of . . ." Ibid., 94.

p. 75, "I advised him . . ." Ibid., 100.

p. 76, "I did not see . . ." Dubcek, *Hope Dies Last,* 113.

p. 79, "an organization with . . ." Havel, *Disturbing the Peace,* 90.

p. 79-80, "I don't believe . . ." Ibid., 98-99.

p. 80, "The Whirlwind the . . ." Ibid., 110.

p. 82, "that week showed . . ." Ibid., 109.

p. 82, "I saw the whole . . ." Ibid., 108.

p. 83, "The main door . . ." Dubcek, *Hope Dies Last,* 183.

p. 83-84, "It came up that . . ." Ibid., 214.

CHAPTER SIX: Normalization

p. 87, "I had written . . ." Havel, *Disturbing the Peace,* 114-115.

p. 87-88, "Palach's death, which . . ." Ibid., 110.

p. 88, "The seventies were . . ." Ibid., 119.

p. 89, "no play took me . . ." Ibid., 120.

p. 89, "the popular term . . ." Ibid., 121.

p. 90, "I think the real . . ." Ibid., 122.

p. 90, "many of our . . ." Ibid.

p. 92, "The laughter and . . ." Ibid., 124-125.

p. 92-93, "the cultural policy . . ." Ibid., 125.

p. 93-94, "For example . . ." Ibid., 124.

p. 94-95, "Why are people . . ." Václav Havel, *Open Letters: Selected Writings 1965-1990*, Paul Wilson, ed., trans. (New York: Alfred A. Knopf, 1991), 52.

p. 95, "most brutal forms . . ." Ibid.

p. 95, "for fear of losing . . ." Ibid.

p. 95-96, "your responsibility . . ." Ibid., 82-83.

p. 96, "as a citizen . . ." Ibid.

p. 96, "a kind of autotherapy . . ." Havel, *Disturbing the Peace,* 123.

CHAPTER SEVEN: The Spirit of '77

p. 97-98, "there was a . . ." Havel, *Disturbing the Peace,* 126-127.

p. 98, "something ought to . . ." Ibid., 128.

p. 98-99, "was not a settling . . ." Ibid.

p. 99, "this was a time . . ." Ibid., 130.

p. 100, "Nemec and I both . . ." Ibid., 132.

p. 101, "could impress upon . . ." Ibid., 135.

p. 101, "were signed on . . ." Václav Havel, John Keane, ed., *The Power of the Powerless: Citizens Against the State in Central-Eastern Europe* (London: M. E. Sharpe, 1985), 217.

p. 101, "basic human rights . . ." Ibid.

p. 102, "does not aim . . ." Ibid., 221.

p. 104, "There were interrogations . . ." Havel, *Disturbing the Peace,* 140.

p. 106, "works only as long . . ." Havel, *Open Letters: Selected Writings 1965-1990,* 141.

p. 107, "the simple longing . . ." Ibid., 156.

p. 107, "A dissident . . ." Ibid., 169.

p. 108, "reading it gave . . ." Ibid., 126.

CHAPTER EIGHT: Living in Truth in Prison

p. 109, "by the very . . ." Havel, *Disturbing the Peace,* 150.

p. 110, "it's true you . . ." Ibid., 157.

p. 110, "there is one certainty . . ." Ibid., 155.

p. 112, "they realized I was . . ." Havel, *Disturbing the Peace,* 158.

p. 112, "That month in the . . ." Ibid., 161.

p. 112, "just imagine—you . . ." Ibid.

p. 113, "the beautiful dream . . ." Ibid., 162.

p. 114, "adjourned indefinitely . . ." Václav Havel, *Selected Plays: 1984-87* (London: Faber and Faber, 1994), 59.

p. 116-117, "Did you sleep . . ." Ibid., 69.

p. 117, "the various interpersonal . . ." Ibid., 68.

p. 117, "you can continue . . ." Ibid., 76.

CHAPTER NINE: The Velvet Revolution

p. 127, "truth, humanity, freedom . . ." Keane, *Václav Havel,* 358.

CHAPTER TEN: The Velvet Divorce

p. 136, "These tactics work . . ." Keane, *Václav Havel,* 358.

bibliography

Dowling, Maria. *Czechoslovakia: A Brief History.* New York: Oxford University Press, 2002.

Dubcek, Alexander. *Hope Dies Last: The Autobiography of Alexander Dubcek.* New York: Kodansha International, 1993.

Keane, John. *Václav Havel: A Political Tragedy in Six Acts.* New York: Basic Books, 2000.

Kriseová, Edá. *Václav Havel: The Authorized Biography.* New York: St. Martin's, 1993.

Havel, Václav. *Disturbing the Peace: A Conversation with Karel Hvizdala.* New York: Knopf, 1990.

———. *Living In Truth.* Boston: Faber and Faber, 1987.

———. *Letters to Olga: June 1979-September 1982.* New York: Knopf, 1988.

———. *Open Letters: Selected Writings 1965-1990.* New York: Knopf, 1991.

———. *The Power of the Powerless: Citizens Against the State in Central-Eastern Europe.* John Keane, ed. New York: M.E. Sharpe, 1985.

———. *Selected Plays 1984-87.* London: Faber and Faber, 1994.

————. *Garden Party and Other Plays.* New York: Grove Press, 1993.

Simmons, Michael. *The Reluctant President: a Political Life of Václav Havel.* London: Methuen, 1991.

Sire, James W. *Václav Havel: The Intellectual Conscience of International Politics.* Downers Grove, IL: InterVarsity Press, 2001.

Tigrid, Pavel. *Why Dubcek Fell.* London: McDonald and Co., 1971.

Wheaton, Bernard. *The Velvet Revolution: Czechoslovakia 1988-1991.* Boulder, CO: Westview, 1992.

Windsor, Philip. *Czechoslovakia 1968: Reform, Repression, and Resistance.* New York: Columbia University Press, 1969.

web sites

http://www.medaloffreedom.com/VaclavHavel.htm
President Bush awarded Václav Havel the Medal of Freedom
on July 23, 2003.

http://www.radio.cz/en/article/58333
Radio Prague has an online broadcast of Havel's play *Guardian
Angel,* along with interviews about the production.

http://www.coldwar.org/
The Cold War museum is located in Fairfax, Virginia, and its
Web site offers glimpses of online exhibits.

http://www.rferl.org/specials/invasion1968/
Radio Free Europe has an online remembrance of the 1968
invasion of Czechoslovakia.

index